CONFIDENCE CREATOR

CONFIDENCE CREATOR

HEATHER | MONAHAN

BOSS IN HEELS

CONFIDENCE CREATOR

ISBN   978-1-5445-0073-7 *Paperback*
       978-1-5445-0074-4 *Ebook*

For my son who has taught me that confidence is not given—it is created. You may have been the youngest and smallest one on the basketball court, but I watched you go out there and go after it like a boss. I am forever grateful for your example.

CONTENTS

FOREWORD

BY CAROLYN COPE

I've been working with Heather for about three years, and it all began by accident. I was hired to work for someone else, but when that person left the company, I was sent to work for Heather. The experience has turned out to be one of the things I'm most grateful for in my career.

A lot of bosses make the mistake of only telling their employees when they mess up or need to perform better. Heather always took the time to give honest and constructive feedback anytime we needed to hear it, and she didn't do it in a way that made us feel like failures. She did it in a way that allowed us to learn from our mistakes so we could grow. She always pointed out ways for us to improve. That's what separates being a boss from being a true leader.

So many women in our industry put so much pressure on themselves to be perfect all the time. We always have to look beautiful, be charming, perform at the highest level, sell the most, and impress everyone. We're so hard on ourselves. Heather has really opened my eyes to the fact that other people may seem perfect on the outside, but everyone has their struggles. Everyone makes mistakes. We all have good days and bad days. We can't beat ourselves up over it all the time. All we can do is learn from our mistakes and apply that knowledge so we can be even better in the future. And honestly, more often than not, the things we beat ourselves up over are things that no one else even notices.

If we stopped exerting so much energy on the negatives and just focused on how to learn from our mistakes and do better the next time, we'd keep moving forward and improve. Strangely enough, what we see as our own imperfections are probably what make people like us even more because those things are what make us memorable and relatable. These are just some of the lessons that I've learned from Heather.

I've come to appreciate how Heather will always have our backs and encourage us as long as we work hard, produce results, and bring good ideas to the table. By doing that, she gives us confidence to keep pushing the envelope, take more risks, and seek out new opportunities. Sometimes all we need is that someone who truly believes in us and supports us in order for us to take that leap and push ourselves. Heather has done that for me so many times. She has helped me become who I am today. Knowing that Heather has my back no matter what has made me fearless, even outside of the workplace. It's given me courage to push myself, make sure my ideas are heard, and to go after my dreams. She's helped me understand that I'm worth something and I can do great things for myself, for the company I work for, and for others around me.

When I struggled with a bullying situation that started to impact every aspect of my life, I asked Heather to help me through it. She gave me great advice and helped me realize that bullies are, more often than not, jealous or threatened by us. Together, we got through it. Now, not only do I know how to not let bullies get in my head and bring me down, but I also have learned to how to intervene when I see others being bullied.

I've been in several tough situations involving men in my life. I've been sexually assaulted and I've been sexually harassed at work. I've always coped with it by telling myself that it just comes with the territory of being a woman—it's just one of those things I have to deal with. But after Heather made me feel like I'm a valuable and necessary part of her team, I started to realize that I didn't deserve to be treated with anything but respect. It is not

OK to tolerate bullying, sexual harassment, or negative comments. She taught me how to take the tough criticism and negative situations and turn them into fuel that makes me work even harder to prove everyone else wrong.

Hearing Heather talk about the tough times she's been through and seeing the positive impact her stories have had on other women has given me the strength to talk about what I've been through with the women in my community. It's crucial for women to have a support system. Women need other women. I now have great relationships with women just like me who have been through similar situations and have had to fight and struggle to get back on track. I used to feel like a victim who was ashamed, but now I feel like a survivor who is strong. Having a support system like that is huge, and I owe it to Heather for helping me find it.

CAROLYN COPE

JANUARY 2018

INTRODUCTION

This book is about my life, but it's not a traditional autobiography. This book is a collection of stories. These aren't glamorous stories that paint me in a positive light. Far from it. In fact, many of these stories are embarrassing and were painful for me to relive, but each and every one serves a very specific purpose. Each story shares a lesson I learned that helped me grow as an individual and as a woman.

I've always wanted to help others who have been bullied, harassed, and feel bad about themselves. I can relate to those people because I was one of those people. When I was young, I didn't have confidence in myself, but that changed as I grew older. That evolution wasn't simple and it didn't happen overnight. It occurred after experiencing a series of tough but extremely valuable lessons. That is one of the reasons why I started my brand. I wanted to pass on what I learned and help other women identify those bad habits and self-destructive behaviors that held me back for so long. When I speak at events, help out friends, or give advice to clients, I talk about my own personal experiences to illustrate various points and show others how to gain more confidence and grow as a person. I always try to pull back the curtain and use my own life as an example. This book is a collection of all those stories.

In the end, there is no one blueprint for success. Every journey is different, but the tools and techniques we all need to get to our individual destinations are very similar. If you are able to utilize just some of the tools and techniques described in these stories, I promise that you will find yourself gaining confidence, overcoming obstacles, and creating the life you want for yourself.

PART 1
· · · · · · ·
CONFIDENCE

CHAPTER 1

REMIND YOURSELF

"Mom, can you write on my shoes?"

That's what my nine-year-old son Dylan asked me at six-thirty in the morning before school. I was rushing around the kitchen trying to make breakfast and get his bag packed before we had to fly out the door and he's asking me to write on his shoes.

"What? Hurry up, we're gonna be late."

I saw that he was holding out one of his basketball sneakers and a Sharpie. I knew he had a game that night but still had no idea what he was talking about.

"What am I writing?"

"I want you to write 'You can do all things' on the bottom

of my shoe." I think he saw the blank look on my face, so he explained. "Mom, no matter how good you are and no matter how talented you are, every once in a while, you need to remind yourself. When you're in a tough spot, you have to remember who you are. You can't feel confident every minute of every day."

I couldn't believe what I was hearing. *How brilliant was this?*

I wrote out the phrase for him in marker on the bottom of his shoe and handed it back to him. He ran off and finished packing his bag while I watched him in stunned silence. I couldn't get over what had just happened. My son taught me the importance of reminders. I literally cried. I was forty-one and still struggling with confidence. It took me years to learn how to believe in myself. He was nine, but he was already capable of creating a confidence safety net that he could turn to for support when he needed it.

At the time, I was the CRO for a radio company. Because of my job and my role in various charities, I was often required to speak in front of large groups of people at functions, but it wasn't always easy for me. I would feel nervous before I had to take the podium. I'd look out over a sea of faces who were all staring at me and I would feel doubt creep in. I would question myself. That's not a comfortable position to be in. Deep down, I knew that I was capable, but there were times when I found it difficult to call on that confidence. Dylan was right. We need to support ourselves during challenging moments. So after that talk with my son, I took a page from his playbook. I started to write little reminders on my shoes whenever I found myself nervous about making a speech or attending a big meeting.

One month later, I was asked to speak at a charity luncheon for an organization called City Year Miami. They mentor inner-city youth to give them the direction they need to get through school without dropping out. Many of those kids didn't have a support system. Many were impoverished and living in dark places. They were just trying to get by. It wasn't easy to have confidence and trust in yourself when growing up in that environment, so one thing I wanted to stress in my speech was that those kids could learn confidence. Confidence is a skill that can be learned and not one that they had to be born with. What better way to prove that, then, by using myself as an example?

At the end of my speech, I told that story about my son and the message he wanted me to write on his basketball shoe. I brought the actual shoe up with me to the podium. I even showed everyone the messages that I wrote on the bottom of my heels that morning. The very next day, I was sitting at my desk at work when I opened up my email and saw that my mailbox was filled with messages from my friends and coworkers who attended the luncheon. They had all sent me pictures of the notes they wrote on the soles of their heels. "I love me!" "I deserve better!" "I can do this!" "I am not alone!" The messages went on and on. The ladies got into it.

Today, I write reminders to myself on my computer. I have reminders that pop up on my iPhone. I hide some inside my clothes and around my house. I even have a picture frame that says "Hello, Gorgeous!" I sometimes forget where I put them, so when I come across one, it will always bring a smile to my face. More importantly, those reminders have a lasting impact. We all need people who pick us up when we're down, but sometimes it's a job that we can do ourselves. Playing a role in our own rescue is the ultimate key. Sometimes it's as simple as having access to reminders.

If you ever see me at an event, you can bet that I'll have a supportive message on the bottom of my heels.

CHAPTER 2

STARTED FROM THE BOTTOM

My childhood was far from idyllic. I was the second of four kids. My mother married young and had kids quickly, but she soon found herself in a bad marriage and with no job. She had the courage to leave but had nowhere to go, so when I was six years old, she moved us all into a trailer behind my grandparents' house in Worcester, Massachusetts. It was a struggle. We did the best we could to get by and had to rely on food stamps to make ends meet at times.

Sports became a way for me to escape my day-to-day life. I fell in love with sports at a young age and started playing softball in grade school. I was good, maybe not the best, but I was good. I pushed myself to be the best pitcher that I could be. I wanted to win as many games as possible. For a while, it worked. The problem was that I never truly believed I was good. I gave others the impression that I had confidence, but deep down, I felt that I wasn't worthy of my success and didn't believe that I could consistently perform at a high level. In most cases, I was able to play well in spite of my own lack of confidence, but when the stakes were raised and the game was on the line, I psyched myself out before even stepping foot on the field. Without even realizing it, I was sabotaging my own success.

When I was twelve, our team reached the finals. I had pitched well all year, so the coach put the ball in my hands at the start of the game. Instead of taking the mound with strength and confidence, I was terrified. My mind raced with worst-case scenarios. *What if I fail? What if I give up a home run? What if we lose and it's my fault?* It was all gloom and doom. Before I realized what happened, I walked the first batter. As the second batter dug into the box, I waved to the coach and signaled for him to pull me out. I told him that I was sick and couldn't play, but I wasn't sick. I was afraid to fail and I felt like a failure. I didn't believe in myself and I didn't think I was good enough, so I gave up. If you think you can't do something, then you'll most likely prove yourself right.

Fast forward six years to my senior year in high school and I had completely shifted my perspective. It was like night and day. Not only was I confident in my ability on the mound, but I also genuinely felt that I had an unfair advantage. No matter what the situation or how far down I was in the count, the odds were always on my side. The reality was, I could throw three balls and I could still have a shot at striking the batter out. How amazing is that? I relished those moments when the ball was in my hand, and I wanted to be in control when the game was on the line. As a result, I frequently performed well in those situations. I decided I could, so I did.

Looking back, there wasn't one moment that changed my perception or got me thinking differently about who I was and what I was capable of accomplishing. It was a process. It happened incrementally over those six years, but there were clear steps taken that helped me evolve into a more confident and effective player who didn't shy away from the spotlight.

1. PRACTICE

It may be a cliché, but practice does make perfect. Confidence is important, but nothing of value can be achieved without hard work. There are no short cuts to success if you aren't willing to put in the effort. I loved the game, so I loved to practice, and I quickly found out that my work ethic was second to none. If I had free time, I would be outside practicing. If I didn't have anyone else to play with, I'd be in my backyard throwing the ball against the side of the house. The more you practice, the better you get. I also became realistic about what I could and could not control. I knew that I wouldn't always be the most talented player, but I could outwork everyone else. That would separate me from the pack, and it did. You improve with hard work and practice. By default, that will build confidence.

2. SHOW UP

Simply put, just try. Experience plays a crucial role. Over the next six years, I found myself in many more challenging situations. They couldn't all be avoided. I had to dive in, and I learned that I could perform under pressure. I could strike a batter out when the game was on the line. I could get a hit with two outs in the bottom of the ninth. Those mini-victories added up over time. So instead of envisioning the worst-case scenarios like I did when I was younger, I would call on those victories when I found myself in a difficult situation.

3. GAIN STRENGTH FROM OTHERS

I can't take all the credit for my transformation. A big part of my evolution and increased self-confidence could also be attributed to my team. From grade school to high school, we as a team went through many highs and lows. We lost our share of games, but we did it together. No one player was ever at fault. I saw players struggle one day and shine the next. I could relate to their situation, and it made me better understand my own situation. It allowed me to learn from the mistakes we as a team experienced over time instead of beating myself up over what I used to consider a failure.

4. ONLY COMPETE WITH YOURSELF

The final step for me was realizing why I was playing and who I was playing for. When I was a kid, I longed for validity and accolades. I had a desire to be the best, but that was because I wanted the respect of others. Instead of being concerned with what I thought others wanted me to achieve, I focused on what I wanted to achieve. I was playing for myself. I set the standard. I set my goals. I didn't compare myself to anyone else or base my idea of success on what another person might have achieved.

Each of those steps allowed me to speak my truth and take the mask off. I would pick up steam and take another step. All the while, I was becoming stronger, smarter, and better prepared. My confidence was built through momentum, and that momentum began with the first step. My softball days are long behind me, but the lessons I learned from that experience stay with me to this day.

CHAPTER 3

PUT YOURSELF OUT THERE

Do you keep a journal?

The process of writing in a journal is therapeutic, but so is reading back over what you wrote. Building confidence is not like flipping a switch. There is no one thing you can do to suddenly become a more confident person. It's a process that develops momentum and builds over time. When reading over old journal entries, you can clearly see that growth and those steps, but journaling can be more revealing than you imagine.

What I found most eye-opening were examples of my own counterproductive behavior. My journal entries had a pattern and a reoccurring theme. It may seem small or inconsequential, but it stood out to me how I never asked for things I wanted unless I received indication that I had a good shot at getting it. In other words, I didn't take chances. I needed acknowledgment or validation from others before trying to do something. I hadn't consciously realized I was doing this, and that left me wondering how many opportunities had passed me by.

The aha moment for me occurred when I was trying to build my own brand and expand my platform by speaking at various events. Back in January 2012, I was the EVP of Sales when I first attended a digital media seminar in New York City. I would return year after year, and I became friendly with the head of the event, Gordon, who was a digital marketing specialist and a consultant for numerous media companies looking to grow in the digital space. He was smart and kind. He took the time to answer my questions and helped teach me about the space when I was a novice. We weren't close, but he was someone whom I called on and who the company I worked for at the time eventually hired as a consultant.

In my journal, I wrote about how I was dying to speak at his next event. I desperately wanted to approach him and ask, but I didn't have the courage. I came close a few times, but I could never pull the trigger and let him know I was interested. Why not? What did I think was going to happen?

Looking back now, it's clear that I didn't ask because I didn't think he would want me to speak at one of his events. That wasn't the only situation. I found countless examples where I didn't act if I didn't think I would definitely succeed. It was shocking for me to read that because I always considered myself a positive person, but I flipped through page after page where I wrote about being floored when something good happened or if I received positive feedback. I know countless men who think the complete opposite. They are literally appalled if they don't get the raise, while I was more shocked when I did get it. Why couldn't I reverse that and be shocked if someone didn't think I did a good job?

After a year of working with Gordon in a consultant role, he attended an event that I was speaking at. After my speech, he texted me and told me that I was a great speaker. That was the reinforcement I needed. Only then did I have the courage to ask, so I wrote him an email. It wasn't easy, but I did it. He declined my request that first year but then surprisingly invited me to speak the following year. My speech went well, and the year after that, he brought me back to take the main stage. That proved to be a great success and a move that helped me out professionally, but it almost never happened because I was simply too afraid to ask. What if he never gave me that initial reassurance?

Sitting around and waiting for validation from others before I take action is not something I'm interested in doing anymore. I know I'm not going to get everything I ask for, but I do know that if I don't go out and try to get what I want, then the chances are nil that things will work out in my favor. It's never easy to hear "no," but I've learned not to think of it as a blow to my ego. It's not personal if someone turns me down. There could be a slew of reasons why things don't work out, and many have nothing to do with me personally. It might just be poor timing.

Luckily, I've learned to change my thinking over the years. I had to put myself out there and approach people even though I was not always comfortable doing that. It wasn't in my nature, but I was able to recognize that it was in my best interest. Taking that first step is not easy, but the more you do it, the more natural it becomes. I didn't succeed every time, but I can say without any doubt that it's much easier to live with the feeling that I did everything I could to succeed than it is to live with the feeling that I might have let an opportunity pass me by because I didn't speak up or take action.

This doesn't mean that you have to throw caution to the wind and put your health or safety in jeopardy. Far from it. It's often the little things that can lead to the biggest improvements. Just take small steps each day. Put yourself out there. Give yourself one goal or one challenge a day. If you're a person who keeps to yourself and has trouble meeting people or being social, your challenge might be to introduce yourself to another parent you see at school drop-off. That's it. It may not seem like much, but I promise you that those small steps will be enough to positively impact your confidence level in only a few weeks. More importantly, it will make this behavior that you once feared become second nature. This way, when you see an opportunity, you will jump on it instead of giving yourself excuses to hold back.

If you don't believe me, keep a journal. Document your thoughts and experiences. Detail your insecurities and the things about yourself that you want to improve. Use these pages as a way to hone your self-improvement plan. Pushing yourself a little bit each day can become a game. A few months from now, go back and read those pages. If you're taking those steps every day to put yourself out there, you will see a difference in your attitude right there on the page. You will notice how far you've come, and you will be proud. Just remember that when nothing is certain, anything is possible.

CHAPTER 4

CLAIM YOUR SUPERPOWER

A few years ago, I took a trip to the Dominican Republic for a yoga retreat. That was a great experience because I was able to meet a lot of very different people, but the person who made the biggest impression on me was Sharon. We had landed at the airport together and somehow wound up in the same van to the hotel, so we began chatting. I noticed that she was insecure and a bit lost, but she was also kind and sweet, so I fell in love with her right away. When she told me that she hated her marketing job and didn't know what she wanted to do with her life other than to get married and have kids, it began to make sense. I understood where she was coming from.

Over the course of the trip, it became clear that yoga was what Sharon enjoyed and she was great at it. When we returned home, we stayed in touch on Facebook and through mutual friends. Only a few months later, I saw that she'd resigned from her job and completed a teacher training course in yoga. She even started teaching a class in Miami Beach. I hadn't seen her since the trip, so I decided to take one of her classes. When I walked in the door, I almost didn't recognize her. She commanded the room but moved in a sweet and delicate way that was inviting and allowed everyone to feel comfortable. She didn't seem awkward or nervous anymore. She seemed at home. It was so clear that she had found her calling. Over the past few years, she has traveled the world teaching yoga. Sharon had the courage to follow her heart, and it not only built her confidence, but it also changed her life.

Sharon had found what I call her superpower, and she had inspired me to find mine. I was stuck in a rut. I told my friend Todd how it felt as though I was floating through life without realizing my full potential. I had no idea how to get myself where I needed to be. "Do something you've never done before," he told me. I laughed at first because it sounded like generic advice, but he was serious. "Get out of your comfort zone and see what you learn from the experience." OK, why not?

Todd suggested I take a stand-up comedy class. *What the heck?* At first, it was the craziest idea I ever heard. I didn't want to be a stand-up comic. I didn't have any free time, and I definitely didn't think I was funny enough. However, the one thing that struck me was how much I didn't want to do it, so I knew that would make it a good confidence builder. I was willing to give it a try, but there was no way that I was going to do it alone, so I convinced my friend Shari to sign up with me. We worked together and had high-pressure management jobs in radio. We also had kids the same age, so our time was limited. Still, I convinced her to tag along by saying that if I could find the time to invest in myself, then she could, too. It worked. She was all in.

There is no way to sugarcoat it—that class was painful. The people were different; maybe a little strange. They were definitely not the type of people whom I was used to surrounding myself with. They were mostly introverts who wanted to come out of their shell, but it made me appreciate my own individuality and how different I was from the others in the class. We did strange breathing exercises where we had to grunt. Some nights we would crawl around on the ground and act like various animals. That was about as far outside of my comfort zone as I could get.

A few weeks into the class, we all had to take turns standing up on stage alone and speaking for a full five minutes. I saw that it was stressful for some, but it gave us the chance to support and encourage others, which was great. When it was my turn, I didn't feel stressed or worried at all. I easily used all of my time and talked about some crazy thing that happened to me after speaking at an event. It felt easy. I realized that I had the ability to speak and tell stories. I guess I already knew that I could do it, but that class allowed me to see that I was able to do it in a way that came more naturally than it did for everyone else. That was one of my superpowers, and I had been downplaying it for years by telling myself that I wasn't as good as everyone else when it came to storytelling. If anything, I spent time actually avoiding my superpowers because I thought it might be frivolous or irresponsible to indulge in something I enjoyed when I should be chasing a paycheck. It took decades for me to realize how wrong I was. The funny thing is that I never would have known that had I not taken that comedy class.

So how do you find your superpower? Like with almost everything, there is no one way. Everyone is unique, but the answer is inside you already. You just have to fish it out. One technique that can help unlock those clues is journaling. I've mentioned it before and I'm going to keep mentioning it because journaling has proven to be an invaluable tool in my own life. Journaling can not only help you chart your progress and see how much you've grown, but it can also help you identify your superpower. When looking back over what you've written, try reading between the lines. Look for patterns. Those patterns will reveal when you're happy and at your best. Those are keys that can help point you in the direction of your superpower.

Don't be afraid to ask for help. Ask friends and family because they are the people who know you best. A few years ago, I was honored to be the recipient of the Glass Ceiling Award, which is given to Florida businesswomen who highlight, mentor, and advance other women while advancing themselves. I was told that I needed to speak about my own "unique value proposition." At the time, I wasn't really sure what to say, so I reached out to people in my personal and professional life to ask them what they thought. The responses I received were fascinating. I was able to see myself through the eyes of others so clearly, and I loved that. Learning what others found unique about me was priceless and also incredibly uplifting.

We all know that person who absolutely shines when they are at work, the person who loves getting up every morning. Why can't that be us? Why can't we put ourselves in a situation where we're using our superpowers and enjoying ourselves every day? The majority of our time is spent at work, so why suffer through that. Take the time to find your superpower. It's different for everyone, and no one superpower is better than another. Invest in yourself. Once you find a way to hone your superpower, it will make you more confident and productive and give you that invaluable feeling of self-worth and success. Discover where you should really be and chase after it as if your life depended on it because, in a way, it really does.

CHAPTER 5

TEN WAYS TO BUILD CONFIDENCE TODAY

Unlike talent, confidence is a skill that anyone can learn. We may or may not have certain talents, and we can work to improve particular talents, but for the most part, you either have a talent or you don't. Skills are different. Skills are like a muscle that can be developed over time. Confidence is a skill that can be learned at any age and in any socioeconomic situation. Confidence is one of the most important keys to building a successful personal and professional life. If this is a weak spot for you like it has been for me, here's how you can get started.

1. FIND YOUR BASELINE

You need to know where you're starting from. We are often blind to our weak areas. I was a very outgoing and competitive kid. I made sports teams and won contests, so many people assumed that I was confident. I even assumed I was confident. It wasn't until I got divorced that I realized I wasn't confident at all. Sometimes something very negative has to happen to get your attention and make you look at yourself clearly. Divorce was that event for me. I felt like a failure, a loser, a quitter, and a terrible mother. That was when I realized I wasn't confident, and I took a closer look at why. *How can I be so hard on myself? Why am I talking to myself like this?* That started me down a new road that has vastly improved my life. Sometimes we really need to fail in order to see what's holding us back. Try to be as honest as possible in your assessment of your confidence level. It's easier to chart where you're going and how much progress you need to make if you know where you're starting from.

2. FOCUS ON YOUR STRENGTH

We all have one. If you're not sure what your strength is, ask a good friend to point it out to you. I promise you that it's there. It might be your warm smile or your empathetic ear. Identify yours and appreciate it as your superpower. Remember all the times your superpower has given you strength and allowed you to rise above. Think of all the times you've succeed while doing something you're good at. You have that confidence inside you already. Build off that and get the ball rolling.

3. BE GRATEFUL

Write down three things that you are grateful for each day. The more time we spend focused on what we are grateful for instead of dwelling on what we're lacking, the better we feel about ourselves and the faster our perspective in life changes for the better. Things are never as bad as they seem.

4. IT'S TEMPORARY

When you hit a rough patch, remind yourself that life is like an ocean. There are times where you're riding high on a beautiful wave and times when that wave comes crashing down. The important thing to remember is that life is a cycle and you will inevitably get back up on that wave again. If you need some occasional help, keep a snapshot of the ocean on your desk to remind you.

5. LISTEN TO YOUR INNER VOICE

I used to think confidence was all about winning, but that's not how it works. If you win or lose, that's just another life experience. Confidence is being able to take a chance and do something that you want to do when you know you might fail. Confidence is having the courage to know you're good enough regardless of your bank balance, hair color, or child's report card. Confidence is feeling good about yourself in spite of those things. I've learned that if I listen to my intuition and then act on it, I will build confidence in myself. That doesn't mean that I'm going to get what I want or win every time. I won't, but that doesn't matter. What matters is being true to myself and who I am. Don't shut yourself out or silence your desires. When was the last time you listened to your intuition and acted on it?

6. BE YOUR BEST YOU

Take care of yourself. I don't mean that you have to focus on looks. I mean put yourself first. Women often have a hard time doing this. They feel guilty putting themselves before their loved ones. If you don't workout, sleep, meditate, relax, or do whatever special things you need to do for you, you won't be the best version of yourself. When you're not your best version of yourself, you can't do things for others. In a way, it's actually selfless to take great care of yourself because it allows you to be more present for your family and friends. You will also feel better, which is a natural way to build confidence. What are the things that make you feel good? Write them down. Do those things every day. Make yourself a priority in your life. No excuses.

7. YOU DON'T HAVE TO BE PERFECT

No one is perfect. If you find someone who is trying to give the impression of being perfect, RUN! Those are the least confident and most insecure people. After turning forty, I've learned that the people who put up a front have a lot to hide. By letting the world see your flaws and imperfections, you boost your confidence and accept yourself. It also draws others closer to you. We are all flawed, and there is beauty in those flaws. We just have to get to a place where we can appreciate them. #workinprogress.

8. PRACTICE

Just like working out at the gym, we need to train multiple times a week to get results. Confidence is no different. Put yourself in the best position for success. That means practicing, researching, and preparing for whatever it is that you're trying to do. If you need to make a presentation at work, preparing at home the night before will boost your confidence in that meeting the next day. If you're nervous about a social situation, researching the best conversation starters and trending hot topics will help you feel better prepared. Whatever the situation, you will feel more confident going in if you prepare and practice. You can't control the outcome, but you can rest easy knowing that you did everything possible to get ready.

9. FAKE IT TILL YOU MAKE IT

This is a standby and it works. If you stand up tall, make eye contact, deliberately shake hands, smile, and put on your best superhero gear, you automatically appear like a confident person. Whether you have it or not in that moment is irrelevant because it appears like you do. People treat you different when they think that you're confident. If I'm given an opportunity at work that I'm not prepared for, I always take it and try to figure it out after. If there is a challenge or opportunity that I'm interested in, I go for it even when I don't have the confidence that I can do it. Confidence is built during preparation and when taking a chance. It's in those moments when I realize what I am capable of. This may seem like backward logic, but I promise you that it works.

10. GIVE BACK

It doesn't have to be a big donation or a time-consuming gesture. It can be something small, like being polite by holding a door. This makes you realize that you are capable of bringing value to others. This can be a powerful realization. If you're feeling low, try helping someone else out. Listen to their problems. They will appreciate you for that. Those confidence builders pop up around us every day. You're the one who has to take the initiative and go after them. Work the confidence muscle daily and watch it grow!

PART 2

. . . .

PERCEPTION

CHAPTER 6

STAY IN YOUR LANE

Working out has always been an escape for me. It made me feel calm and helped relieve my anxiety. When times were tough, I'd go running. When things weren't going well, I looked forward to my daily workout.

Once I moved to Miami, I started working out at Barry's Bootcamp, but I quickly learned that the gyms in Miami were much different from the gyms I was used to. The thing about Miami Beach is that all of the women look like supermodels in their twenties. If you've ever been there, you'll know that I'm not exaggerating. When you're the type of person who compares yourself to others, Miami can be a difficult place to live. I was one of those people at first. I was older than most of the other women in the class, so I had plenty of reasons to doubt myself. It was intimidating, and that hurt my progress and my own self-worth. Suddenly, the one thing I loved wasn't so fun anymore.

Over time, I got to know a few of those women. I knew that I didn't look like Gisele, but I quickly realized that I had more personality and heart than those other women whom I was putting up on a pedestal. I slowly started to realize that being me was pretty great. I wasn't going to let myself be intimidated, and I wasn't going to let my insecurities ruin something that I had come to love.

"Stay in your own lane"—that became my mantra. I meant that figuratively and literally. We'd start each workout by running on the treadmill. Mirrors lined all the walls of the gym, so I made sure to not look down the row at all the attractive young women. I'd look dead ahead in the mirror and try to psych myself up. *I love you! I love you for being here and getting through this workout.* I visualized myself growing so strong that I could take off into the sky. I had evolved to a place where I focused entirely on myself and visualized where all my hard work was taking me. All of the people around me on the treadmills faded away. It was such an uplifting experience that I couldn't wait to get to the gym every day.

Stay on your own treadmill. The other treadmills are already taken, and we have no idea what steroids, coaching, or genetic mutations others have, so let's not compare ourselves. Comparison is the greatest thief of all joy. When you stay focused on you, the view is much better!

CHAPTER 7

THE ONE-WEEK CHALLENGE

I stopped comparing myself to others at the gym, but Barry's Bootcamp helped shine a light on some other negative behaviors that were hurting my confidence and preventing my growth. I shifted my perception so I felt empowered on the treadmill, but as soon as we moved to the floor to lift weights, everything changed.

I found myself scrambling between thirty different people trying to get weights. At times, it was chaotic and stressful. One day while making the mad dash, I caught myself saying "Sorry" over and over again. It hit me. I just went from a situation where I felt empowered to a situation where I felt like I was in the way. *What other times do I feel that same way?* I realized that it didn't occur only at the gym. I had been apologizing to everyone including my friends, family, spouse, son, coworkers, and even strangers. On the surface, it may not seem like a big deal, but the signal I was continually sending myself multiple times every day was that I was a secondary member of society. Yet again, I was holding myself back.

Men tend not to make this same faux pas, but as women we will apologize for everything. What we're really doing is making our own needs less important than the needs of others. We don't even realize we do it, but it's a habit that we've created and accepted over time. When I was in the Apple Store waiting to buy a charger, I noticed the female greeter kept saying, "I'm sorry you had to wait so long." Why does she need to apologize to me because it's busy in here? I caught myself apologizing to my son's teacher when I wanted to ask her a question. Why was I sorry that I had a question?

Once I realized how many times I would apologize over the course of a normal day, I was actually mad at myself. That was bullshit! The madness needed to stop. The next day, I decided to make a change. When I made the transition from the treadmill to grab the weights, I would say, "Excuse me," instead. I wasn't going to just stop with that situation in the gym. I would apply it to my entire life. I turned that into my own one-week challenge. For seven days, I would not allow myself to say I was sorry in social situations when I had nothing to be sorry for. I armed myself with some phrases so I would be ready in an instant.

Simply saying, "Excuse me," instead of "I'm sorry" was a small but significant change that immediately made me feel empowered again. My conversations at work and with those closest to me changed as well. I didn't feel secondary anymore. That shift put me in the driver's seat.

One ancillary benefit was that it was also a way for me to unload a lot of unnecessary guilt that had been building up. My family lived in Seattle at the time, so we didn't get to see one another often. I was constantly asked by my mother why we couldn't fly out to visit. I would love to bring my son to visit my mother, but it wasn't always practical. Traveling for work was beyond challenging, and when I got home from a business trip, the last thing I wanted to do was get back on a flight. However, that's not what I used to tell her. Instead, for the past decade, I would apologize that we couldn't make the trip. When I hung up, I was left feeling guilty. I decided instead to shift the conversation: "Mom, as I'm sure you can understand, work travel is wearing me down, and I'm not able to get back on a flight again. However, I would love to have you all come visit us."

Simple shifts in the conversation allowed me to step away from feeling guilty and offer up another solution. When they would decline because the trip expense would be too much or they weren't able to take the time, I would simply say, "I completely understand. Travel is so difficult and costly." Done!

The impact that had on me was one that I immediately wanted to share, so I decided to write a blog post about the topic. One of the responses I received blew me over. One woman said that my intent was spot-on, but that there was an even more powerful response that I could use. "Try thanking people instead of apologizing." We've all been late for a meeting or an appointment before. It happens. Instead of stressing out and apologizing, why not walk in and calmly say, "Thank you, everyone, for your patience. Let's get started." Wow! That's amazing! In those situations, my first response had always been to blame myself and then to beg for forgiveness.

I recently had a deadline to get some papers signed and sent back to a vendor. I was unable to get my legal to approve and sign off in time, so instead of shifting into apology mode, I decided to give a different response in my email. "I know that you had requested the contract changes today. Unfortunately, our legal has been unable to get to our document and won't have it completed until tomorrow. Thank you for understanding, and I look forward to having this matter resolved then."

By thanking instead of apologizing, we imply that our comments will be accepted and we are grateful. This is the most badass way to handle a situation that I can think of. I'm still practicing this one and definitely getting much better at it. If you're a person who frequently apologizes, try taking the one-week challenge. It will open your eyes to behavior you weren't even aware of. Stop relinquishing your power. Take it back!

CHAPTER 8

ENEMY NUMBER ONE

When did I start beating myself up in my mind?

I have no idea. I remember giving myself a verbal beat-down back in fourth grade when I quit the school play, so that behavior has been ingrained in me for a while. I have been my own worst enemy for as long as I can remember.

It doesn't matter if you're in fourth grade or forty years old, if you constantly tell yourself things like, "I can't do this," or "This will never work," or ask yourself questions like, "What was I thinking?" you've already created a reality where you can't succeed. This can happen without anybody else influencing your mindset. You may think that nobody knows what you're thinking, and that may be true to an extent, but our thoughts deeply impact our own self-worth. While I may not have said all of the awful things that were in my head about myself publicly, I certainly shared a watered-down version of things like, "Oh, I'm so stupid," "I can't believe I did that," "I'm such an idiot," or "Blonde moment." The list goes on.

One day, out of the blue, I got a call from my friend Colleen, whom I had known since I was fifteen. I was in her wedding, and I remain close to her and her family today. Everyone has that one successful friend who seems to have it all together, the one who never gets into trouble and manages to do everything right. That friend for me is Colleen. We both had a strong work ethic and commitment to fast-tracking our success. Colleen had a great job at a high-profile consulting firm. She would always motivate me to be better and push myself to advance. Having a wing(wo)man in a similar situation always yields new and interesting perspectives to learn from and apply to our own life. During our conversations, we usually recapped our week and discussed how we could get ahead. That day was a little different. It had been brought to her attention that the self-deprecating comments and quips that she occasionally made were negatively impacting the way others saw her.

Colleen and I grew up taking shots at ourselves and considered it normal. It was flippant and seemed harmless, but neither of us had any idea the impact that it would leave on others. When I heard her story, I immediately knew that I was guilty of the same thing. I panicked. *What did the people I work with really think about me? What kind of impression was I giving off?* I had always thought that poking fun at myself made me more relatable and down to earth when, in reality, it made me appear like someone with low self-worth.

From that moment forward, we both decided to put an end to that behavior. If I made a harmless mistake, it was healthy to laugh it off and move on, but I was no longer going to take shots at myself at work. While it's not easy to break old habits, it can be done. The decision to stop making myself the butt of jokes at work made me appear to be a more confident person who respected myself. Therefore, I commanded respect from others.

I had stopped putting myself down at work, but it wasn't until years later when I realized that I still kept that nasty habit alive in my personal life. I had been talking to my Brazilian friend Elaine about how I thought I looked terrible that day. I think my actual comment was, "I feel like a ten-pound sausage in a five-pound bag." She was shocked. She looked at me like I was crazy. I was so used to saying those things that I thought she was the one who was nuts. I rolled my eyes as I prepared for her to tell me that I looked beautiful and blah, blah, blah, but surprisingly, she took a different approach.

"Please tell me that you never say that in front of anyone

else," she said. I wasn't ready for that. Nobody ever said that to me before. It turned out that in Brazil women don't put themselves down or ask others if they look fat in certain outfits. Instead, no matter how they may feel, they exude confidence and embrace their inner diva. All the Brazilian women I knew appeared so sexy and confident. They must be onto something.

Changing that behavior was a no-brainer, and it was a quick fix. If I didn't want people to think I was an idiot, then I wouldn't call myself one. If I didn't want other people to think I was out of shape or unhappy with my body, I wouldn't plant that seed in their mind. Not only did I stop speaking about myself in a negative light, but I also chose words to describe myself that I wanted others to use when describing me.

The easiest way for me to observe that change was through my fiancé's eyes. Having been together for years, he was painfully familiar with all the various issues I had with my body on regular occasions. He had spent so much time over the years correcting all of my negative comments that it became his job to talk me up before we went out together. That couldn't have been fun for him. Now, I no longer have to ask if I look fat. I don't even think it. Instead, I walk out ready to go, and he says, "Wow, you look great!" I thank him with a sly smile or wink. That creates a positive vibe at the start of our date nights. I also notice that the act of *accepting* the compliment, and not challenging it, makes me feel more confident.

The most important voice and opinion in your own life will always be your own. The good news is that your voice and opinion is the easiest to change because you are in charge of it. It's so simple, but so few of us do it. Speak about yourself the way that you want others to speak about you, and they will. Take action and implement the change. Learn how to channel your inner Brazilian goddess and you will emerge a goddess in your own life.

CHAPTER 9

BE NICE TO YOURSELF

It's one thing to speak about yourself in a way that you want others to speak about you, but it's another thing to really believe those things you're saying. It was easier for me to stop making negative comments about myself because I didn't want others to hear me say them, but it was much harder for me to stop having that negative dialogue with myself that no one other than me ever heard. That took much more work and commitment to correct.

It turned out this was something else my son was able to help me with, even though he was too young to realize it. Dylan was born on May 31, 2005. I was working at a radio company and living in Miami Beach. I found it incredibly stressful trying to juggle my career along with my duties as a new mother. Many nights, I would give myself a pretty severe inner beatdown. My marriage was failing, and I was angry that I might be making decisions that would leave my son growing up in a broken home. Those days were dark, and aside from the joy I felt about being a new mother, I was not a happy person.

I would tell all of that to my shrink, Gail. Finally, one day she asked me, "What kind of example are you setting for your child? Would you speak to your son the way you speak to yourself?" Of course not! I would never do that, but children learn from their parents. It pained me to think of my son growing up to be the type of person who thought of himself the way that I thought of myself. I didn't want him to beat himself up. I wanted him to learn how to forgive himself for his mistakes.

That was another epiphany moment for me. That enemy inside me was resilient and would strike in ways that I didn't always notice at first. I thought I had outsmarted it for the time being by changing the way I spoke about myself to others, but it would still rear its ugly head internally. For the past thirty years, the person who was the cruelest to me was actually me. It was a vicious circle that I had simply gotten used to.

Once again, I decided to start down a new path. I would treat myself with the same love, kindness, and forgiveness that I would treat my son. In order to kick that up another notch, I wrote out a list of words I wanted to use when having that internal dialogue.

Kind

Loving

Empathetic

Smart

Talented

Charismatic

Funny

Beautiful

Interesting

Creative

I read that list every night before bed to remind myself of all of the wonderful traits that I had. Problem solved, right? Well, not really. I wish I could tell you that it was all that simple, and I magically thought of myself in a new, positive light, but nothing is ever that easy. Honestly, it all felt phony at first. I sort of knew that I was trying to manipulate myself, but I kept at it because I also knew that if I didn't truly forgive myself, nobody else would. I kept updating that list with real-world examples to reinforce those words on the page. Sometimes I needed evidence to really believe it. In time, it began to sink in, but I was still far from perfect. I'd often catch myself getting frustrated or beating myself up. In those situations, I would stop and remind myself of all my special and unique attributes. Slowly, that nasty inner dialogue ended. Those realizations helped me make big changes in how I saw myself. It wasn't magic and it didn't happen overnight. It happened with practice. It happened because I made that a part of my nightly routine.

Once I escaped from that toxic mentality, I was able to focus on what I wanted for my life. By deciding to be my biggest cheerleader instead of my number one saboteur, I not only shifted the way others would see me just by my word choices, but I also shifted how I saw myself. I now choose words to describe myself that are flattering and positive, and others respond positively to it. I do, too.

We all have the power to make this change. If you don't have a child, think of your pet. Would you speak to your pet the way you speak to yourself? Would you speak to your niece or nephew like that? Create a conversation with yourself similar to the one you would have with those who are most special to you. When you begin treating yourself as one of the most special people in your world, you will begin to emerge as someone who deserves to be treated that way by everyone.

CHAPTER 10

TRUTH VS. REALITY

In 2016, I traveled to New York City to appear on Cheddar TV. It was an interview segment about how women could position themselves in the workplace and become their own best advocates.

Before shooting began, I walked onto the set and met the two bombshell hosts. They were both significantly younger than me and looked like they just walked off the catwalk. That left an impression on me, and not a positive one. I immediately ran to the bathroom to reapply as much makeup as possible. I had made the mistake of trying to compare myself to them physically—an endeavor destined for failure from the get-go.

Ego wounded, I returned to the set, and the interview began. I couldn't help but feel self-conscious at first, but as soon as they started asking me questions that I knew the answers to, I found my groove. Whenever I'm doing something I know I'm good at, my superpowers take over and my nerves eventually melt away. The interview became effortless, and I shared my story about ending the need to apologize.

As soon as we wrapped, the girls asked me if I would help them because they both struggled with their confidence. *What? Really?* That was such an eye-opening experience. I had been comparing myself to them and falling very short when in reality they were dying to learn what experience had taught me. The entire time they had been looking at me with admiration. *How did I not see this?*

This is something we all do. When in these situations, we all create stories in our own minds, but sometimes the opposite is true and we can't see it because we're too caught up in our own self-doubt. It's so easy to focus on the negative, but things are not always what they seem on the surface. The next time you find yourself in a similar situation, don't let the negative thoughts taint your outlook. Every time a negative thought pops into your head, force yourself to counter it with the opposite possibility. The more you practice the techniques in this section, the more positive traits you'll be able to pull from your saddle bag in time of need. If doing what you have always done has gotten you where you are today, it is time to take a chance on doing things differently.

CHAPTER 11

LOOK FOR THE SILVER LINING

Back in the late 1990s, my life seemed perfect on the surface. I was living with my boyfriend, Derek, in Massachusetts. I was a healthy young woman in her twenties with a fantastic house and a successful career in sales. I was succeeding, but somehow I was not happy. I felt empty. I didn't know what was wrong with me. At that time, I never thought to meditate, journal, or lean on my friends for help. Instead, I suffered in silence.

I knew that I didn't have the answers, but while I was out walking my boyfriend's dog, I thought of a person who did—Oprah! I needed to get in contact with Oprah. She would know the answer. She would know what I needed to do to fill that emptiness inside me. And I'm not joking either. I actually tried to call Oprah. When that didn't work,

I did what I did best at the time—I laid blame elsewhere. I was not ready to accept responsibility for my life or my choices. I had no idea that I could empower myself to live the type of life that I wanted, so nothing changed.

A short time later, I had gone away for an overnight trip with my girlfriends. I couldn't reach Derek when I was gone. That was one of those moments when I knew something was wrong. I was waiting for the bomb to drop and it did when I arrived home the following day. I walked into the house where I lived with Derek and found the place trashed. It was clear there had been a large party the night before. I found a T-shirt with lipstick on it in a pile of soaking wet clothes in the laundry bin. Someone had gone swimming in their clothes with my boyfriend and I knew it was a girl. I knew he cheated on me, but of course he denied it. I packed up my things and stayed with my friend Stacey. Over the next couple of weeks, I was able to wear Derek down and got him to finally admit that he cheated.

I was devastated and had no idea what I did wrong to end up in that situation. I went into work each day wearing flip-flops and the most depressing clothes I could find. I couldn't pick my head up, and I reeked of sadness. Working became an escape. I threw myself into my job and tried to work harder than everyone else. It was at that time when my boss, Jon, approached me and asked if I would get on a plane with him for an equity opportunity unlike anything I could ever imagine. He wouldn't tell me where I would be moving to but said that it would give me the chance to build my reputation in a new market while establishing myself as a leader.

The idea of picking up and moving someplace completely different to start over sounded terrifying, but I was not happy where I was and I needed a change, so I decided to step out of my comfort zone and take a chance. Heartbroken and at my lowest, I boarded a plane with Jon, and we landed in Michigan. Yup, Michigan. If I was looking to jump-start my career, I probably would have chosen a city like Los Angeles, New York, or Miami, not Michigan. But a commitment is a commitment, so I stayed and worked. I learned a lot while working that job, and there were some very tough lessons. That time in my life was not a happy time, but it was one that I drew tremendous strength from because I finally learned that I was capable of overcoming challenges without support from others. That made me feel strong, and it built up my confidence.

That breakup, which seemed like the end of the world, set in motion a series of events that led me down a new path—a path that would ultimately lead me to a place where I would find my answers. It's easy to get comfortable and convince yourself that you're content in a situation that isn't healthy. By breaking free from the status quo, you open yourself up to meeting new people and creating change, which leads to opportunity. Looking back now, it's clear that everything unfolded exactly how it was meant to. When you're going through difficult times, keep an eye out for the silver lining. It might not be obvious at first, but there is always a way to learn from a difficult situation and grow.

PART 3

. . . .

ADVERSITY

CHAPTER 12

LEAPFROGGING VILLAINS

Everyone's story has a villain. There are those who support you and those who try to pull you down. You will never be able to root out all of the villains in your life, so learning how to leapfrog those villains is essential in becoming successful.

I wasn't in corporate America very long before I realized that not everyone was a good person. I was naive and never imagined that people who didn't know me would try to hurt me or hold me back for no good reason. I learned quickly that villains in the real world don't wear witch hats or ride a broom. Some villains are sneaky and fly under the radar. They look like normal people. Some are meek and quiet; others are affable. But all of them are fake on some level. You have to keep your eyes open so you can spot those villains.

I encountered my first professional villain very early in my career. I had just graduated from college and had no idea what I wanted to do, so I went to work in the wine business as a salesperson. I liked it and I was good at it. I was doing my job and trying to be the top salesperson in record time. I didn't realize that someone was out to get me. I heard from friends that Jenny, another salesperson, was bad-mouthing me to other employees in the company. Aside from a few brief encounters, I didn't even know the woman, so I had no idea why she had any ill will toward me. It didn't make sense, so I decided to ignore her.

The more you elevate yourself and succeed, the bigger a target you become for potential villains. When I became the top salesperson on our team, Jenny became increasingly vocal in her disapproval of me. She was attempting to poison others with stories of why people shouldn't like me. She went so far as to go to leadership and tell them that I was a poor representative for the company.

Ignoring a villain can be a good first step, but I've learned that most villains need to be sent a much stronger message and be confronted head-on. The Wicked Witch needed a bucket of water thrown on her to make her disappear. Ignoring her wasn't enough. When the situation with Jenny escalated, I needed to find my bucket of water.

I thought back to a lesson my former boyfriend Ned had

taught me years earlier. Ned was a police officer who, because of his job, had a habit of preparing for the worst-case scenario in every situation. One thing he used to always warn me about was jogging outside alone. I loved to run, but Ned explained how I needed to pay attention to my surroundings so I could react in case of an emergency. It was important to run in neighborhoods that were populated and had lots of light. He also warned me about dogs. I thought he was kidding, but he had a point. What do you do if a dog gets loose and chases you down? You have only seconds to react. A lot of people try to run away and get hurt, which is why Ned told me to do the opposite. He said to run at the dog and yell at the top of my lungs. It seemed crazy, but it made sense. The idea was that I needed to prove I was the dominant one. A few months later, I found myself in this exact situation when I was out running. A rottweiler broke free from a nearby fence. The dog came barreling at me and looked like it wanted to tear me apart. I wanted to run, but I remembered what Ned told me, so I started screaming and pointing my finger at the dog while running as fast as I could right at it. I got within feet of the dog when it suddenly began to whimper and turned back toward the house with its head between its legs. I couldn't believe it. Once I caught my breath, I nearly fell over.

Jenny, my fellow salesperson, posed a much different threat than the dog, but I had to deal with her the same way—head-on. My opportunity presented itself when she asked for a private meeting with me. I didn't want to take the meeting, but my boss encouraged me to meet with her and get it over with. Up until that point, I had avoided her because the whole thing was ridiculous and annoying, but keeping my distance only allowed her to spread more ill will and grow in strength.

When I walked into the conference room, Jenny was sitting at the head of the table looking stoic and cold. I sat down across from her, and she proceeded to explain how she felt there was tension between us. *Huh?* I didn't feel the tension. I just felt annoyed that she was bad-mouthing me, but I sat there and heard her out. She went on and on about what it takes to succeed in a man's world. She felt that the way I carried myself was not conducive to making it. I had to ask, "What do you mean?" She told me that the way I dressed was unacceptable and that I was bound to fail if I didn't dress more like her. Now, Jenny was ten years my senior and had an entirely different look and style than I did. She had a short bob and wore pants to work every day. She wasn't someone who had much of a feminine side— at least she didn't show it at work. I, on the other hand, favored skirts and had long hair that I wore down every day. I very much embraced my femininity, and the way I dressed gave me a sense of strength and empowerment. It was a key step that helped me build confidence. I wasn't going to give it up because of that woman.

I had heard enough. It was time to throw my bucket of water. I told her that I was not her. While she may favor pants and short hair, I did not. I liked the way I dressed, and the way I wore my hair was not a problem. It clearly wasn't a problem for anyone else because I had just been named the number one salesperson in the company. With a stern look, I asked her, "Is there anything else? I need to get back to work."

That was it. It wasn't an easy conversation for me to have, but she had been shut down. Slaying that villain made me feel stronger. A situation that had been uncomfortable was resolved. From that point on, she backed off and kept her distance. Speaking your mind and defending yourself may seem like a simple step, but it's a surprisingly effective one when you're in the right. Most villains like that aren't used to being confronted or called out for being wrong, so doing so puts them in an uncomfortable position. Don't sit around and wait for someone else to do it for you. You are your own best advocate, so it makes sense that you are the most qualified person to slay your own villain. Practice what you're going to say. Prepare answers for certain responses. If you stay calm and respectful and speak your mind, the message will be sent loud and clear.

CHAPTER 13

THE IMPORTANCE OF
INFORMING OTHERS

Sometimes villains are the last people you suspect.

After moving to Michigan, I didn't know anybody outside of work, so when I heard that Bob, my former coworker, would be transferring to Michigan and working with me, I was excited to have a familiar face around. Bob and his wife, Denise, moved right down the street from me. Things were great. The three of us saw a lot of one another on nights and weekends.

One night, Bob and I had to take our biggest client into Detroit for an auto show. We rented a limo and spent the day seeing the cars and learning about new technology. At the end of the night, the limo driver dropped the client off at his house first. Bob and I lived fifteen minutes away.

We were alone in the back of the limo when Bob rolled up the window divider between us and the driver. At first I was confused. "What are you doing?" He ignored my question and told me how lucky he was to work with me and how much fun he had with me whenever we hung out. It was awkward, but I didn't expect what happened next. He pushed himself on me and tried to kiss me.

I pushed him off me. I was shocked. Then I was pissed. I couldn't believe he had the audacity to do that. His wife was my good friend. In fact, they were the only two friends I had in Michigan. I tried to get some answers, and he went on some rant about how his marriage was not good and that things weren't always what they seem. He said his wife wasn't happy, and he wasn't sure how much longer they were going to remain in Michigan. Blah, blah, blah. The car ride lasted a lifetime, but we eventually made it to my house. I was able to remove myself from one of the most uncomfortable situations I'd been in. I went inside and cried. I knew that I would no longer be able to be around Bob and Denise.

I wanted to call Denise and tell her what happened, but I didn't. Instead, I waited until the morning before I called my boss. I explained to him in detail what happened and told him that I wanted to quit because I could no longer work with Bob. I should have told him to fire Bob, but I wasn't that confident yet and thought it would be better if I just got out of there. Luckily, my boss didn't want to hear any of that. He wouldn't let me quit. Instead, he caught a flight out to Michigan.

In the meantime, I ignored Bob at the office. I didn't have the courage to say what I really wanted to, so I just kept quiet. Today, I know better, and that situation could have been awful for me, but luckily I had a good boss at the time who took the initiative and moved Bob out immediately. Denise and Bob soon left Michigan, and I never heard from either of them again.

Part of the reason why I never spoke out was because I used to think that standing up for myself meant that I had to yell and be a bitch, but that's actually not true. Standing in my power and expressing my anger over being treated poorly doesn't have to be a fight. Standing up for myself can be done without emotion and done from a place of strength and calm.

Today, I handle these situations differently. Years later, I was giving out an award at an NAB event when we hit a snafu on stage. I learned that the award I was giving out was to be received by the one company that boycotted the event. I was able to think on my feet and quell the thousand booing people in the audience. I turned a negative situation into a positive one, so I walked off that stage feeling elated. My good friends had taken great pictures of me on the jumbotron, and we were off to the lounge to celebrate. I couldn't have been happier, but on my way to the ladies' room, a man grabbed my arm. He said something about how it must be so tough to have blond hair and fake boobs. He said more, but I didn't hear him because I was struggling to break my arm free from his grasp. I was able to get away and slink into the bathroom. I was terrified, and at that moment, I never wanted to go up on stage ever again, but I eventually realized that that was a knee-jerk reaction. I regrouped and made my way back to my crew. I told my friends what had happened. Not only were they able to put the situation in perspective and make me realize that the man's hatred had nothing to do with me, but they actually chased him down in the lobby. Ten minutes later, he apologized to me for what he'd said. It turned out that my friends were right all along because the man had just lost his job and hated those who appeared to be succeeding.

I refuse to roll over anymore. I may not be able to solve every problem that comes my way, but I have a great group of friends I can turn to when I need help. Today, I can speak up and leave anger out of it. I use my voice to defend myself. If I feel I'm being wronged, I do something about it, so I go from being the victim in a situation to an empowered woman. I can tell you from experience that nothing feels better. This is a sure-fire way to build your confidence muscle.

CHAPTER 14

SEXUAL HARASSMENT IN THE WORKPLACE

What happens if your villain is the person you work for?

I was promoted in the wine business a few months after my face-to-face conversation with Jenny. I had a great opportunity, and I began working closely with the company president, Charlie. He was the leader and the type of person who commanded the room when he spoke. He was clear and direct and had charisma. The team loved him, and he loved the team. I was excited and honored to be singled out by Charlie.

He would message me during the day. That was not unlike other bosses I had before, but soon the messaging became more frequent. At first, I chalked up the added focus and attention to my position being new. He then started to ask that I meet him for face-to-face meetings outside of the office. That was odd. I mentioned it to my other boss, Matt. He agreed that it seemed strange but encouraged me to stay professional and do my job. Hopefully, it was nothing.

I went to those outside meetings and nothing bizarre happened. I tried to ignore my gut, which was telling me that something was not right. I talked myself out of believing there was any issue and convinced myself that I was being overly sensitive. I loved where I worked, and I was proud of my promotion. I told myself that I should be flattered that the president of our company was taking such interest in my success.

Never ignore your gut. Slowly, the tone of the messages began to change. *What are you wearing today? When can I see you again?* I couldn't tell myself that the messages were professional or innocent anymore. I went to Matt and asked for help. That put him in a difficult situation because he also reported to Charlie. I knew Matt was a stand-up guy but found out later that, at that time, he started to look for other opportunities outside the company. He knew something that I didn't yet understand and that was how the culture of harassment at any company is virtually impossible to stop when the leader of the organization is the source of the problem. Matt suggested I document every interaction I had with Charlie.

I was sad. It felt like all of my recent success was hollow. Nothing I had been telling myself about my work being appreciated was true. I was hurt that someone would treat me with such disrespect and disregard. I felt trapped, so I spoke to some of my girlfriends. To my surprise, they all had similar stories of being harassed by someone at work. For something that was so common, nobody ever wanted to discuss it. I guess that was also part of the real problem. If nobody was talking about it, it was like it wasn't happening. I knew I didn't want my boyfriend at the time finding out. Who knew what he would have done? So I kept quiet for months and kept documenting the incidents like Matt had told me to do.

Things didn't get better. They got worse. The messages became more frequent and more inappropriate, so keeping track of everything made it feel like a second job. It felt like Charlie had become obsessed with wanting to know where I was at all times. Documenting my interactions with Charlie was a negative experience that made me feel worse because it was a constant reminder how real that whole thing was. It wasn't long before I was exhausted. I couldn't take it anymore. I couldn't bear the fact that my boss had become so focused on me. That also began to create space between me and my boyfriend, so I finally had to tell him what was going on. The job was no longer worth it. I took the journal I'd compiled and brought it to the owner of the company along with my resignation.

Quitting a job is never easy, but in my case, it was necessary. I'm not saying that this is always the best course of action because everyone's situation is different, but I truly believe that cutting negative people and situations out of your life is like removing a weight from your shoulders. It enables you to move freely and make room for positive opportunities. Shortly after leaving the company, I attended an event with my boyfriend where I struck up a conversation with my soon-to-be boss who'd hired me on the spot.

It took my getting out of a bad situation to understand how much harm I was doing by staying there. Unfortunately, sexual harassment happens in every field. One of the most important things I've learned over the years is that predators like my former boss often prey on younger women who are not confident enough or don't have the resources or experience to properly handle the situation. As I've grown older, these situations have become less frequent. At the time, I did the best I could. Part of me wishes I had sued to show other women how to stand up for themselves, but I didn't have the courage to take that on back then and I certainly didn't have the confidence.

Sharing my stories and being open and honest about my experience today is the next best thing I can do to help other women feel that they are not alone. We need to do this today more than ever. The #metoo movement has gotten me thinking about how we grow a movement so it can ultimately change culture. This is no small undertaking, but it's something that needs to happen. And it won't happen with a couple of celebrities coming forward. It has to happen through each and every one of us. We have to find our voice. We have to put ourselves out there. Most importantly, we have to help one another.

Mentors are hard to come by, and I didn't have one in my younger years. Today, I have a few mentors, and they have helped me make massive changes in my life for the better. Much of my success can be attributed to mentors believing in me and challenging me to grow. Why can't we all make the commitment to do the same for others? Unfortunately, there are too many people who are insecure and don't want to help people. They put on a mask and smile but won't go out of their way for someone else. Those are some of the people holding back our broken culture and preventing it from flourishing.

Mentoring others is not a completely selfless act. I never anticipated the reward I would receive from being a mentor, but I have found profound joy in playing a small role in helping others overcome obstacles and stand up for themselves. In life, we get what we give. Sharing our stories and letting people know that they aren't alone will result in more people speaking out about injustice. The stronger we are as a unit and the louder our collective voice becomes, the more likely we are to change the culture. Speak your truth because you are not alone.

CHAPTER 15

SHINE A LIGHT ON SHAME

We all make mistakes, and I am no exception. Unfortunately, sometimes we get ourselves into trouble and create adversity that makes our lives more difficult. This can be humbling and embarrassing and lead to setbacks, but you have to dive in and deal with it the same way no matter how difficult it may seem.

Things were looking up when I moved from Michigan to Florida and started a new job. A month into the job, I was focused on forging relationships, so I set up a dinner with our largest advertiser, Ben, who owned a number of car dealerships in the area. At dinner, we shared wine and had a great conversation before going our separate ways at the end of the evening. That was long before Uber, so I drove myself home after dinner. I was pulled over two blocks away from my house. The officer asked me if I had been drinking. I told him that I had. He let me know that

I was speeding and that he was taking me to the station. I had never been arrested before, so I was freaking out. I had no idea what to expect.

When we arrived, I was brought into a small room with no windows to wait. A few minutes later, two male police officers entered the tiny room. One made inappropriate comments about how I looked and what acts I could perform in order to be released. Yes, that really happened. In that moment, I felt powerless and realized that I could be assaulted or worse. My survival instincts kicked in. I backed against the wall and told them what I was going to do when I got out of there. I was not going to go away quietly, and I would make sure that he couldn't do what they were doing to anyone else. Then I started to scream. The first officer didn't seem phased, but his partner was clearly not comfortable with what was happening. They briefly argued and then left.

A female officer escorted me into another room. I had my belongings taken. I stripped down and changed into an orange jumpsuit before they put me into an enormous holding cell. There was one toilet in the middle and a group of women lying on the floor. I was mortified and scared. I sat in the corner and literally rocked back and forth for what felt like an eternity. I was finally given a chance to make a phone call, so I called Ben to come get me out of jail. Hours went by. Nothing.

Finally, I heard a tap on the glass. A female officer called me over. She asked why I was there. She told me that there was no reason why I should still be in jail and asked why I hadn't left yet. I told her exactly what happened with the other officer. It would take some time, but she discovered that the officer who harassed me didn't put me in the system. Ben showed up to bail me out but was told that I wasn't there. Luckily, the female officer fixed the problem. I phoned a bail bondsman and was able to get myself out of that horrible situation.

After being in jail for twenty-four hours, I got home and took the longest shower of my life. I had no friends in Florida at the time. I had no idea what I was going to tell my boss. I made up my mind that I was going to resign. Up to that point, that's how I dealt with problems, but when I called my boss, he had a different idea. Knowing people who had been in similar situations, he suggested that I stay. He wanted me to be candid with my employees. "Tell them what happened and answer their questions," he told me. Yikes! That was almost as bad as quitting. I wasn't looking forward to it. I was embarrassed, ashamed, and disappointed in myself, but I held a sales meeting and shared my story with the team the following day.

Once again, my worst fears proved incorrect. A number of people appreciated my honesty and shared similar stories from their past. Up until that point in my life, I had no idea that shining the light on my own shame made telling my story and moving forward so much easier. The experience actually made me more relatable to my team and helped me forge some lasting friendships. My first instinct had always been to run from my problems and hide from my shame. I've learned not to run from my mistakes because I would be running my whole life. It may not be comfortable, but take ownership of the things you do wrong. You might be surprised by the result.

CHAPTER 16

KARMA

In the end, I believe that people get what they deserve. It may not seem like it sometimes, and you don't want to sit around and wait for others to fight your battles for you, but sometimes the universe has a weird way of working itself out.

I had just been named the VP of sales at a radio company, so I was riding high and feeling proud about my recent accomplishments going into the company's annual awards night. Part of the event was a roast. That was my first year at the company awards night, so I had no idea what I was in for, but I was warned about an employee named Tommy who would roast other employees. I didn't know Tommy, and I couldn't imagine why he would attack me, so I didn't think much of it.

Being the youngest member of the leadership team, I

was both excited and a little nervous about the event, but I showed up smiling. Then Tommy took aim at me. During his routine, he called me the "new VP of cleavage." I thought the comment was beyond inappropriate. I was crushed and mortified. People were laughing, and I did my best to muster a laugh because I thought that was the best way to handle the situation. Boy, was I wrong. I was not throwing a bucket of water on my villain. I let the water get thrown on me. My confidence hit rock bottom. I struggled not to cry, and I had to excuse myself from the table. I went to the ladies' room where I broke down.

Afterward, I called my old boss who was one of my biggest supporters. I told him what happened. He encouraged me. He went so far as to say I should sue Tommy. He told me to quit, and we'd figure something out. More importantly, he had my back. The following week, I let my boss know that I had a problem with what happened and didn't want to be involved in a roast like that again. It wasn't supportive. It was hurtful, and I deserved better. That was something I needed to do. Speaking our truths and standing up for ourselves allows that confidence muscle to grow again. My boss listened to me, and Tommy never took aim at me again.

What goes around comes around. A few years later, I found myself sitting through another awards meeting, complete with another roast. Tommy got up and did his thing, but he made sure to avoid saying anything about me because he had been told I was off limits. Tommy never considered that at one point someone might roast him. That night, we had invited a guest performer looking to break into radio to serve as our entertainment. That performer turned out to be a very young Taylor Swift, and she was sitting at my table with her mother. A couple of minutes into the roast, she leaned over to me and said, "Are you kidding me? This guy gets away with trashing everyone else?" She was horrified. Before I could respond, she jumped up and ran out the door. I thought she left because she didn't want to listen anymore, but she returned ten minutes later after speaking with other employees and getting dirt on Tommy. She used that as ammo to roast him through a song she performed on stage. Taylor Swift won my heart that day, and she definitely threw that bucket of water on Tommy that I never did.

We are all in control of our own destiny and responsible for our own success, but if we stay the course and do the right thing, every once in a while, karma will have our backs.

CHAPTER 17

THE COMEBACK IS ALWAYS BETTER THAN THE SETBACK

Setbacks are unavoidable. They come in all forms, and more often than not, they come unannounced, which makes them impossible to anticipate or prepare for. Setbacks can be crushing, but how you conduct yourself and how you choose to respond is one of the ways that will determine your character.

There is nothing more exhilarating than making progress. A year ago, I was starting to come into my own at work, in the gym, and in my personal life. I was empowered, and it felt like nothing could stop me. As a person who had already been living life very fast for the past ten years, those victories only intensified my pace. Not taking time to deal with stress, not resting or even relaxing can really wear you down. It will eventually catch up with you. If you aren't listening to the universe and paying attention to the signs, the universe will hit you over the head to get your attention.

I received my message from the universe loud and clear. I had just gotten home from a work trip. I was rushing to the gym so I could get a workout in before I packed my suitcase and picked up my son so we could meet my fiancé at the airport. His daughter was playing water polo for the Junior Olympics team, and we were all flying down to Peru to watch her play.

I had been tense all day. I could feel my back aching on my way to the airport but figured it was just stress from work and would go away soon. Everything seemed normal when we boarded the plane and took our seats, but I quickly realized I couldn't get back up. The slightest movement came with a shooting pain. If you've thrown out your back before, you know that pain is like no other. I say this after having had a C-section, knee surgery, and both my gallbladder and appendix removed. None of those other things compared to the pain I felt in my back during that flight.

Knowing that I was stuck on that plane and unable to move for hours, I did what anyone would do: I decided to throw back cocktails in an attempt to numb the pain. I've since learned that dehydration only compounds the problem, so I was slowly making it worse. By the time we landed and got to the hotel, it was midnight and I could barely walk. I don't think I slept one minute that night. I lay in the hotel room bed with ice covering my back and waited for morning.

The next morning, I made it to the game but had to stand up and lean against a pole the entire time. Any attempt to sit was met with excruciating pain. After the game, we all went to the emergency room. The emergency room in Peru was much different than what I was used to in the United States. Nobody spoke English, which was scary when you don't speak Spanish. My fiancé had to translate every word for me. As the minutes passed in the waiting room, my son became more and more worried because he had never seen me hurt before. We finally got in to see the doctor who wanted to take an X-ray and also set me up for an MRI, but when they tried to get me out of the wheelchair and onto the gurney, I screamed so loud that it scared the doctor. My son lost it. "Help her! Help my mom!" My fiancé tried to keep everyone calm, which only upset my son more. Suddenly, tears began streaming down my face and I couldn't stop crying. It was scary being in another country and not knowing if I was receiving proper medical care. It was frustrating not being able to communicate with anyone, and it was painful watching my son suffer. Finally, the doctor gave me a shot for the pain and inflammation before sending me to get an MRI.

I had an MRI in the United States before, but the protocol was much different in Peru. I had to prep myself to sit in the tube for a half hour without moving so they wouldn't have to start over. *You've done this before. You'll get through it again*, I had to keep reminding myself. I pictured myself lying on a beach in the sun. The mental images helped me get through that half hour and eventually back to the hotel. It turned out that two discs in my lower back were rubbing against each other, so I was forced to stay in bed for the remainder of the trip. It was not a good time. On the flight back to Miami, I lay down and counted the minutes until we landed. I couldn't wait to see an American doctor and start getting better. Soon after I landed, I got in to see the doctor and started rehab almost immediately.

Physical therapy was not what I'd expected. When I arrived, they took me into a private room where I had electrodes hooked up to my back. It was very relaxing and passive. I knew I was in good hands and felt that I was starting down the road to recovery, although there was a part of me that wondered if I would ever be back to normal again. No longer able to work out, I suddenly didn't have the release that I had grown dependent on, so my stress level was at an all-time high—not helpful when you're trying to relax. After my first session, I walked through the office and noticed that the majority of the patients were much older than me. Some were permanently in wheelchairs and attended therapy to work muscles that they would otherwise never move. Reality slapped me in the face. Seeing how much worse the situation could be gave me a strange sense of appreciation. Instead of being upset, I suddenly felt gratitude.

Each week, my therapist, Alex, would record my mobility and pain level. She charted my progress so when I would get down on myself for not improving fast enough, she would go back to my chart and show me how far I had come. Seeing how my pain level decreased over time gave me hope that I was going to fully recover. I felt proud. Progress is a funny thing. It's difficult to track while you're going through the daily grind. It isn't until you finish and look back that you can really see how far you've come. I started showing up at physical therapy ready to work. I no longer went to relax. I worked out hard to strengthen the muscles in my back. More than anything, I wanted to run again. Running had always been a freeing form of escape. My best ideas came to me when I ran. I solved problems when I ran. I was able to access something so special when I ran, so having that taken away from me was devastating.

One day, Alex pointed to a strange-looking machine and said she was ready for me to get in. I didn't know what it was at first, but it was a machine that allowed me to run without supporting all of my body weight. There were pants that I had to zip myself into before the machine filled up with air so my back could withstand the pressure from running. I hadn't been able to run in so long, and finally being able to again made that feel like such a magical experience. I thought of all those people still confined to their wheelchairs and felt like the luckiest girl on the planet.

I started working out on my own, and pretty soon, I didn't need to return to physical therapy. I missed seeing the people who worked hard each week and put in the time and energy to feel happy, even though they would never get out of their wheelchairs. I also missed seeing Alex and having her track my progress, but the experience taught me valuable lessons and made me a much stronger person who was better prepared to tackle life's challenges.

Today, I track my own progress. I know that there is a solution to every problem even if I haven't found it yet. Just because you can't see it doesn't mean that it doesn't exist. Ride that wave. When you're on the bottom, the one thing we know for sure is you will get back up on top again. Take a step back and realize the wave is just a part of life and try to enjoy the ride.

CHAPTER 18

REDIRECTED, NOT REJECTED

I was on the road to recovery from my back injury. I was feeling better. Nothing could bring me down. Then I got fired.

It was Tuesday, and I was on a work trip in Los Angeles when I received an email from my new CEO saying that she wanted to meet with me that Thursday morning in her office when I returned. I knew something was wrong—not because she wanted to meet, but because she was so nice to me in the email. That woman was never nice to me. It was going to be ugly. I tried to reschedule because getting there for the meeting required me to take a six-hour flight on Wednesday and then drive three hours in the car, but she told me that I needed to be there regardless.

I knew I was walking into a bad situation. I spoke to my fiancé, and we decided that if she was going to fire me, I would say as little as possible and leave as soon as possible. I didn't realize that the meeting was going to be only a couple of minutes long. After fourteen years of leading the sales organization and being an executive at the highest level in the company, she simply told me that my position was being eliminated. I could sign a paper saying that I resigned, or she was going to let my team know that I had been terminated. I knew it was going to be bad, but that caught me off guard. I had just been recognized as one of the 40 Most Influential Women in Radio, and now I was getting fired. I told her that I wouldn't sign or agree to anything. I didn't want to resign, and I had no idea why any of this was happening.

Walking out of that office was hard. I felt that I had been treated so poorly and felt used. It felt like something had just been taken from me for no reason at all. The next twenty-four hours would be the toughest. I cried the entire ride home. I was not only defeated and discouraged, but I was also exhausted. I had never been fired before, so the situation was completely new to me. The uncertainty was terrifying. That feeling morphed into anger and disgust the next day. That whole week was a roller coaster of emotion. At times, I was crying because I was so upset, while other times I almost felt happy to be away from such a negative situation. I knew that one day, I would be OK; I just had no idea when that day would be. My fiancé and son were great during that time. They helped me to create a "no negativity zone" at home to make sure that I remained positive. Without their support and encouragement, I don't know where I'd be today.

It took about seven days for the volatile roller coaster to come to an end. I began to get some much-needed clarity. I had already changed my phone number and bought a new phone so I could start over. It wouldn't be easy, but I knew that I needed to reach out to others, so I made the following post on social media: *After fourteen years with Beasley Media Group, leadership has eliminated my CRO position. I want to thank my team, partners, clients, and all of the amazing people whom I have known over the years. It has been an emotional few days, and I wanted to thank everyone for their love and support. If I have impacted you in any way over the last fourteen years, please leave me a comment below. I would love to hear from you. Thank you!*

That changed everything. Some people were shocked that I would post something like that. I figured people would find out anyway, and if I didn't reach out, I wouldn't be able to get any help. By the following day, I had received a tremendous amount of encouragement and made some great new connections. The comments on my social media were amazing! What I enjoyed most was how people shared with me their own stories of how they overcame adversity after being fired.

My friend Elaine shared a story with me about being unhappy with her job at a salon. She worked at one of the biggest salons in Miami Beach, but the owner was a terrible woman who was awful to her employees. It was beyond draining, so Elaine put her foot down and was promptly fired. She was petrified and didn't know what to do next, but suddenly, the clients started to call her. She would go to their homes to cut their hair. She doubled her income the first year and opened her own business the following year. She made sure to tell me that if she hadn't been fired, she'd still be working for a nasty person and not living her dream life. That gave me hope, and it truly lifted my spirits when I needed it the most. My mindset was beginning to change. A week earlier, I was petrified, and now suddenly I was hopeful that things were going to work out for the best. Those responses were huge. Even today, I will often go back to read some of those responses because they move me so much.

Many of the people who responded also offered to help. The easy thing for me to do would have been to ignore that, but I decided to take advantage of it by asking them to do one specific thing for me. That might be making a connection, writing a letter of recommendation, or even just advice. By making one specific ask, those who were offering were now delivering. That helped me piece together a plan. I tracked my progress. I made a grid that I hung on my wall so I could go back and look at how far I came—just like I did when recovering from my back injury. That was a game changer because I found strength in that progress. Up until that point, I had been the person others relied on for help, but now the roles were reversed. I felt painfully vulnerable at first, but the experience brought me closer to my friends and family.

There were plenty of roadblocks that first month. One big one was having to change my old company profile on my LinkedIn account. I desperately wanted to change it, but I didn't know what to write. That may seem simple, but I wrote thirty different versions of my profile and still couldn't get it right. I called friends to see what they thought and was encouraged to just write a draft up on the platform. If I liked it, I could save it. Little did I know that when you begin rewriting your profile, it simultaneously appears on your page for all to see. I guess my rough draft was good enough to go live. In the end, I had agonized over that and wasted so much time. When in doubt, sometimes the best course of action is just to take action. Don't hesitate. It turns out that I still have that same profile on my account to this day.

Suddenly, I felt a whole new sense of freedom. After a lifetime of doing what I thought I had to do, I was in a position to do what I wanted. That seemed so foreign, yet so exciting. Instead of working for a paycheck and consuming myself with that work, why not decide where I wanted my life to go? Who knew when I'd get that opportunity again? At the same time, I was under pressure. I did not have a paycheck coming in for the first time in my life. Being someone who had worked since they were twelve years old and was used to being the primary breadwinner, that made me nervous. I had a son to take care of. That panic can drive you to take a quick job and essentially trade one bad situation for another. I was getting offers, but I wanted to hold out long enough to make sure my head was right and my confidence was rock solid before I made a decision. Being terminated reminded me that confidence is not static and needs to be built up again when it is weakened.

Things were looking up in my third week after being fired. I felt better and was able to think clearly. I was also removed enough from my job to see things from another point of view. How much had that toxic work environment impacted me physically and mentally? Over the previous year, my hair started to thin, but it was suddenly starting to grow back. I started to realize how that negative person was like an anchor weighing me down. My body was sending me signs that I needed to get out of that situation, but I hadn't been listening. It started to make sense. Only after I'd shed that anchor was I able to take off. I was finally getting the chance to do what I was meant to do. I was getting the chance to soar.

After my fourth week, I was presented with amazing

opportunities. I had been asked to appear on a television show, consult for a company, and even endorse a brand. No longer did the future look bleak. I was actually excited about what the future had in store for me. The fear had slipped away. The roller-coaster ride had finally come to an end. More importantly, I was back to looking at things in a positive light. I didn't focus on the anger or hurt feelings that came with being betrayed. Instead, I focused on all the new opportunities that were coming my way. If anything, I was overwhelmed by hopefulness. I was in the driver's seat, and the ability to create my dream job seemed like a very real possibility.

Getting fired came as a blow that I was not prepared for. It felt like I had lost everything, but I realized that they couldn't take away the reputation that I had built over the past twenty years or the work I had done. They couldn't take away my network. They couldn't change the quality person I had become or the confidence I had in myself.

It's funny how the uncertainty that felt so scary at first had become exhilarating. Instead of focusing on all the negative things that could happen, I shifted my perspective to focus on all the possibilities that would allow me to change my life for the better.

Some of the greatest success stories began with an unexpected firing. Oprah Winfrey was told she wasn't right for television and was fired. She turned that setback into an opportunity to create a brand that transcends all others. Mark Cuban was fired from his sales job, and that termination allowed him the opportunity to go out on his own. J. K. Rowling was fired from her admin job because she was too creative. While unemployed, she began to write. Sometimes it takes being down and hitting bottom to realize that doing what we want doesn't have to seem so unrealistic. Have faith that there are better days ahead. Speaking from someone who has been there, I can tell you that it's true. I am constantly reminded that life isn't about what happens to you; it's about how you respond in the face of it.

CHAPTER 19

TURNING TRAGEDY INTO TRIUMPH

A little over a month after being fired, I heard that a former coworker of mine was fired from the same company. I called him immediately, and he sounded so scared and sad. I understood how he felt because only four weeks earlier I felt exactly the same way. I told him what I did and how I got back on my feet. Over the past year, people have shared with me their own personal stories about getting fired and how they dealt with adversity. I started compiling those stories and put together a list of techniques that helped me and others get through difficult times like these. When people tell me they've been fired, here is the advice that I give them.

FEEL SAD

First and foremost, it is necessary to give yourself some time to feel hurt, upset, and angry. I certainly felt that way. I cried for two days straight. Anytime you suffer disappointment, you will struggle. Don't skip this step. Don't pretend you aren't feeling these things. Let it out because it's the first step you need to take in order to bounce back stronger.

HAVE A THIRTY-DAY PLAN

I broke my plan down into weeks. Each week, I had specific goals I wanted to accomplish, and each week was a step that helped me to get to my ultimate monthly goal. Everyone's goals are different, so come up with a plan that fits you and what you want to accomplish. Write it down because seeing it in writing makes it visual and makes it real. Crossing the days off on a calendar helps, too. You will see yourself getting closer to your goal and feeling better. Most importantly, have faith that things can change for the better.

KEEP A JOURNAL

Write down what you're doing each day. Write down how you feel. List your fears. Describe what actions you want to take each day to improve. When you set a goal to lose weight, you weigh yourself each day to keep track of your progress. It's no different when you find yourself trying to get through a difficult situation. It's the equivalent of taking your temperature each day in that it allows you to see how you're getting better, even if you don't initially feel any better. This will become your road map to rebuilding your strength. At the end of this process, the insight you glean from your notes will empower you in ways you can't imagine.

REMEMBER THAT YOU'VE BEEN HERE BEFORE

It may sound depressing at first, but identifying another time in life when you have been hurt helps. After I was fired, I went back to look at my divorce journal to see where I was at different times and how I progressed to eventually move beyond the pain. You gain strength by reading how you previously overcame adversity. It reinforces the idea that you can do it again.

EXPRESS GRATITUDE

Shifting your perspective and expressing gratitude will help you to accelerate your progress and get you closer to your goal of feeling better. Every morning when you wake up, write down three things that you are grateful for. It can be something substantial such as your children, friends, or health, or even something smaller such as a good hair day or a beautiful flower you saw on the way to your car.

Taking the time to stop, look, and appreciate the beautiful things in life will give you plenty to be grateful for.

DO WHAT FEELS GOOD

Take the time to enjoy songs, smells, walking, exercise, being outside, separating from technology, meditating, and spending time with those you love. Find out what makes you feel good and do it. The more time you spend doing things that make you feel happy is time well spent.

OPEN UP

Sharing what happened to you with others is huge. You will be shocked to learn how many people want to help you and want to be there for you if you simply ask. If you share your own story, people will share theirs. Put yourself out there. The universe has a funny way of giving you what you need, but you can't sit back and expect it to fall in your lap.

LOOK FOR A SILVER LINING

Getting fired was like a punch to the gut, but after some time, I realized how my stress levels had decreased. I was calm. I was not rushing around. I was happy to wake up each day. I was able to appreciate my son and fiancé and see how absolutely amazing they truly were. Both of them continue to blow me away with their support.

LIVE IN THE PRESENT

It's so easy to get ahead of ourselves or get anxious when thinking about the uncertainty of the future. Don't fall into that trap. You want goals and you want to work toward those goals, but live for today. Realize that you are living in the moment and the moment is yours. You are exactly where you need to be. Anything is possible today.

CREATE YOUR OWN FUTURE

Use words that encapsulate how you picture yourself in the future. Create visuals in your mind to make it feel more real. Write down your goals and desires so you can be reminded. Spend some quiet time seeing yourself where you ultimately want to be and feeling how you want to feel. Watch the universe rise to help you get there.

TAKE A STEP BACK

Think about your former goals. Do you have the same goals today that you did years earlier? People change, and as they do, so does what they want. It's easy to put on blinders and race toward a goal without realizing that deep down inside, you might have shifted lanes. You might not want the same things, but continue to pursue those same goals because that's what you've always done. What are you meant to be doing? What will it take for you to get there? Take this time to reassess and modify your goals so they better fit the direction you want to take your life.

YOU ARE PRIORITY NUMBER ONE

You are the one going through this, and you are the one who is going to improve your life as a result of it. No one else can do it for you, and nobody has to give you anything. You have to work for it, and you have to be your biggest supporter. That all begins with putting yourself first. Before every flight, the attendants go through their spiel and explain how during an emergency you must put your oxygen mask on first before helping others. This doesn't mean that you should turn your back on others, but you have to survive before you can help others. Start your survival strategy today.

BE OPEN TO SIGNS

Notice what is happening around you. Sometimes the answers to the most complex problems have simple solutions that were right in front of us all along. And when all else fails, remember that this is temporary. When you are down, the key is to remember that things will go back up again and nothing is ever as bad as it initially seems. Like most of you, I have had my share of breakdowns, but looking back on it all now, I've come to realize that my biggest breakdowns led to my biggest breakthroughs.

CHAPTER 20

BOUNCING BACK FROM DIVORCE

Getting fired is one of the worst things that can happen in your professional life, while getting divorced is one of the most difficult things to endure in your personal life. Having gone through both, I can say that the feelings of being lost, alone, and worthless were very similar. It's no surprise that the way to bounce back is also similar. Those same techniques that will help you get back on your feet after losing your job will work when going through a divorce or personal challenges. The personal recovery and healing process is similar.

Divorce obviously has some additional complications that make getting through the process more difficult. One of those complications is getting divorced when you have children. My son was one year old when I got divorced.

No matter how upset or angry I felt during that time, I had to put my son first and chose to work my hardest to have a good relationship with my ex. That was not easy and we certainly still have our moments, but I believe that both of us working to treat each other with respect has impacted our son in a positive way. Those early years were challenging. They got better for us, and they will get better for you, too. Keep the focus on yourself. Things will improve if you behave admirably and make good choices. By having my son in my life while going through a divorce, I learned that doing the right thing was not always the easy thing. Making tough choices are never easy, but they will pay off in the end.

Another question I'm frequently asked about divorce involves finances. This is such a common question that my advice was featured in a recent *USA Today* article.

DIVORCED WIPED ME OUT FINANCIALLY. HERE'S HOW I BOUNCED BACK

by Tamara Holmes

USA Today, May 25, 2017

Life took an unexpected detour for Heather Monahan, 42, when she found herself divorced with a 1-year-old son in 2009.

"Financially, I was wiped out as a result of my divorce agreement," the Miami mom says. Compounding her situation, the condo she had purchased for top dollar in 2005 was under water and her job as a sales executive was stressful due to company cutbacks.

Though her financial challenges seemed insurmountable, Monahan eventually forged a path ahead. "I knew that if I continued to work hard and put my nose to the grindstone and tune out everything else I would find a way out of my situation," she says.

Losing a spouse to divorce or death can not only scar you emotionally, but it can wreak havoc on your finances. But there are steps you can take to pull things together and move forward while you also heal your heart. Here's how Monahan regained her financial footing:

Set small goals. Rather than focusing on paying off her entire credit card balance or building her bank account back to pre-divorce levels, Monahan set lower goals that she could complete in a short amount of time. For example, one goal might be to save $1,000. Another was to be at a point where she was not living paycheck to paycheck. Each time she achieved a small goal, she felt empowered to go after a slightly larger one. "All of these were little small wins that helped me feel better about my situation."

Freeze discretionary spending. Monahan gave up buying things like clothes she didn't need and expensive meals. When there was something she needed to spend money on, she looked for a way to do it without incurring more debt. For example, when she wanted to prepay for her son's schooling, she sold her engagement ring to pay for it up front.

Use creative financing. She looked for alternative ways to do things without spending money. For example, it was important to her to take her son on vacation, so she used points from work travel and stayed with friends rather than pay for expensive flights and hotels.

Keep a financial journal. Keeping a positive mindset about her finances was critical. To keep her mood up, Monahan kept a journal where she documented progress, such as paying a certain bill or increasing her savings by a certain amount. When she felt discouraged she would read the journal to remind herself of her progress. "You feel a lot better about your situation when you can see and visualize that progress."

Increase your income. Rather than simply focus on cutting back, Monahan "was able to create more and better financial opportunities for myself via my job."

Today, Monahan says her condo and her bank account

have both rebounded, but she's most pleased about the example of resilience she has been able to share with her son Dylan, now 9.

"I'm proud that I was able to withstand that time and ride that wave," she says.

CHAPTER 21

IT'S OK TO BE SINGLE

Divorce is hard, but for those of you going through the painful process of divorce, please remember that it's OK to be single. It may not seem that way at times, but after going through a divorce and coming out the other side, I understand the pressures. That pressure to be married is very real and often painful. Even if you haven't been divorced, the societal pressure to get married is always there and never easy.

Over the years, I've seen friends excel in their careers and forgo relationships and the opportunity to have children. I've seen friends get married and dedicate their lives to their families. I've had friends who were left by their husbands and others who never found the love of their lives until they were in their forties. What has become obvious to me is that you need to worry about making you happy. Lead the life that you want to lead because you can't plan or dictate how things will play out in the future no matter how hard you try. Those people who put their own health and happiness first are the ones who end up winning the game of life. Taking responsibility for where you are and who you are is empowering. Not everything will work out like you plan, but being empowered puts you in control. You don't need to look to others or wonder "What if?" It's incredibly liberating when you learn that the only person who can get in the way of living the life you want to live is you.

I recently spent time with a great friend of mine who was struggling through a divorce. She was feeling scared, lost, and down. When you think that you're going to be married forever, it's normal to be left with a feeling of hopelessness when it all comes crashing down. Something I've also noticed is how she's becoming stronger because of her divorce. For the first time in a long time, she's pursuing her own interests. She's traveling and spending time with friends instead of focusing on her husband. She may not see it yet, but she's liberating herself, and by focusing on herself instead of someone else, she is moving into a better place.

I used to think that people who put themselves first were selfish, but now I see that they are confident and strong. The better we take care of ourselves, the better we can take care of others and enjoy our lives. This doesn't mean that you have to get divorced in order to be free. I have another friend who has been happily married for twenty years who constantly reminds me to pursue my life and not lose sight of my passions. She continues to work even though she doesn't have to. She credits much of her success in marriage to not giving up on her career and her life outside of her family. No matter what your situation, you have to remember to put yourself first.

What makes you happy? What are your passions? If you knew the world was going to end, what would you do differently today? Seek and you shall find. Once we begin doing the things we love, we put ourselves in a better position to lead the lives we want to lead. Every day is a chance to meet someone new, try something different, and put joy into our lives and the lives of others. It doesn't matter if you're single, divorced, or married. Those are just labels. It's up to you to create the life you want to live. When you forget about all the pressures and preconceived notions, you open the door even wider for that special someone to come into your life. Cheers to you living the life you choose!

PART 4

· · · · · · ·

FEAR

CHAPTER 22

THINGS ARE NEVER AS BAD AS THEY SEEM

Fear is a liar, and that is a fact.

This was a foreign concept to me years ago. When a friend of mine said that I needed to try new things, I told her I was just too scared. Feeling scared is normal. Fear can cripple some people. Think of how you can drive 70 mph on the freeway and subconsciously change lanes without having to strategize about the position of the other cars. Ironically, when you do strategize and overthink, the task becomes more difficult. The same is true about fear. You can get to that place where you subconsciously race toward fear without agonizing over all the little things that can go wrong. It will take some practice, but you will get there if you work at it.

Once again, your journal will be the key. Tracking my small wins has allowed me to tackle bigger challenges. When you decide to ask someone out on a date or speak up in a meeting, you're taking a chance. It's critical that you record those small steps. Regardless if the outcome was what you desired, you need to ask yourself, "Am I still alive?" "Did I die while navigating through that uncomfortable situation?" This may seem obvious, but reading about how you survived fearful moments in the past will take the pressure off. Whenever I'm fearful of a work or social situation, I remind myself that my goal is just to live through it. That's it. When you lower expectations on yourself, you remove the pressure and take some power away from that fear monster threatening to consume your thoughts. Simply trying to do something new is a win, and tracking those small wins will help build strength in that muscle and prepare you for the next encounter. The more small successes you can get under your belt, the better prepared you will be for more significant challenges. The only thing that can stop this forward progress is not trying. Doing nothing is the ultimate fail.

You can start today. Make a list of all the things that scare you, and commit to facing one small fear each day. It could be standing up for yourself at work, or it could be explaining to your spouse that you don't want to go out with their friends on Friday night. Take it on. Don't put any extra pressure on yourself by expecting things to go perfectly. Just do it. It won't kill you. Write it down. That will be a win and the first step toward success. If you do that every single day, those wins will add up and become more significant.

I like to carry around a piece of paper that lists my three favorite wins: the moments when I stared fear in the face, raced toward it, and came out on the other side a better person. One win on that list that means the most to me involves my fiancé. When we first started dating, I put him on such a pedestal. I was crazy about him. After getting divorced, the dating scene was overwhelming. I felt so lucky to find an interesting, smart, kind, and loving man who also loved sports. A new relationship is amazing, but it can also be terrifying if you don't know where you stand with the other person. My strategy when dating had always been to pull away and not show how I felt until after I had been given the go-ahead from the other person. I would try to play it cool and act aloof until the man professed his love for me or made some grandiose display. Only then did I feel safe in letting him know how I felt. That was not a recipe for successful dating, and my relationships didn't work out because the other person assumed I wasn't interested. That clearly wasn't working for me, and it hadn't worked for a while. It made me challenge the way I handled myself in relationships. I was committed to finding ways to show the real me and show how I felt when I was ready and feeling it, not wait for the man to tell me how he felt first.

A few months into my dating relationship with my now fiancé, my good friend Nikki was getting married in California. I wanted so badly for him to come with me, but I was petrified to ask. We got along so well and were having such an amazing time that I didn't want to scare him away by taking what might be interpreted as a big step. He was recently divorced, and I didn't know what he would think of my asking him to take that trip—and to a wedding of all places. At the time, I wasn't used to taking chances like that or racing toward fear. I was a beginner and I needed help.

When I brought my son over to my friend Jill's house for a play date, I told her my dilemma. She agreed to help, and together we crafted a text, which she made me promise to send. Honestly, that was as stressful as deciding what college to attend. I panicked. If I messed our relationship up, it felt like the world was going to end. The fear that had built up in my mind wasn't real, but it had consumed me and driven me crazy. Fear can trick you into believing the worst-case scenarios that run through your head. That's why it's so important to understand that fear is a liar. It's not real. The sooner you know this and believe it, the sooner you can navigate these situations with a clear head.

Jill took my phone and sent the text. I hid in the bathroom until he responded. I have no idea what I was hiding from, but I couldn't be anywhere near my phone. My confidence was at an all-time low because I never put myself in situations where someone could say no to me. I had no idea if I could handle hearing no. Right when I started to convince myself that the relationship was over, I heard Jill call me from the other room. "Come on out! He responded!"

I don't even remember leaving the bathroom. The fear was so crippling. I just remember reading the nicest response. He told me that he wanted to go with me to California but couldn't because he had his kids that weekend and suggested that we make plans the following weekend to do something special. Crisis averted. Had I never taken that chance and sent that text, I would have never known how he felt. That was the first time I ever put myself out there and let someone know how I felt without knowing how they felt first.

Eight years later, I am so glad I sent that text. Today, we are engaged. It's hysterical to think that I once doubted this man's feelings. There was never a chance that he wasn't in love with me. Apparently, it was obvious to everyone else, but unless I saw a helicopter overhead with a sign saying it was so, I wasn't convinced. Thank God things have changed. While every day hasn't been perfect, I am definitely myself with him. Putting a stop to that game I used to play of pretending not to care was the best thing I ever did for our relationship and for me. I am so glad I took that step because I've come to realize that he probably wouldn't have taken it without my lead.

Taking action in your life is like setting a series of dominoes in motion. If that first one doesn't fall, none of them fall. You can't win every time, but taking chances pays off. Each time you face your fear makes it easier to do again.

CHAPTER 23

EVERYONE NEEDS A GOOD WINGMAN

Growing up, I never really knew my biological father. He had been in my life when I was very young, but after my parents divorced, we had limited contact. By junior high, I no longer knew how to get ahold of him. My mother had remarried, and my new father had adopted us. It felt like my biological father had never existed. That seemed easier than dealing with the reality that this person had disappeared from my life.

Over the years, friends would ask me about my father. I introduced my stepfather as my dad. The fact that we had forged a good relationship seemed good enough for me. That worked until I was in my late twenties and I found myself at a crossroad. I had been living in Naples, Florida, and working at a radio company. On the outside, things seemed great, but something was missing and I didn't have the answer. I came to realize that I needed to find my biological father and fill in that missing part of my life that I had ignored for so long.

The first person I called was my sister, Stacy. Stacy is my older sister and the only person I could talk to about that. She was very supportive, and even though she had no burning desire to search for our father, she didn't want me to feel alone. Once she gave me the green light, I began to search online and found an old address for Bill Monahan. That address led me to a number that eventually allowed me to get in contact with his neighbor who agreed to leave a note on his door with my contact information. A few days later, I received a call from an unknown number. I panicked. I knew it was him and I was terrified. It took everything inside me to answer that call, and I still don't know what compelled me to answer, but I did and I'm proud of myself for taking that step.

To say the call was awkward was an understatement, but I asked if Stacy and I could meet him, and he agreed. We set a date. Stacy flew to Naples, and together we drove to meet him. I was nervous. No, I was petrified. Petrified that it wouldn't go well. Petrified that he wouldn't like us and also petrified that we wouldn't like him. At that age, I was insecure and I wanted to back out, but thankfully my sister kept me talking the entire car ride.

When we pulled into the Outback Steakhouse, it felt like my heart was going to explode. My blood pressure must have been through the roof. From the car, Stacy and I could see our father sitting inside the restaurant with his wife and son. We had known that he was remarried and had a child, but we didn't know they would be there. I watched my father from a distance. He looked small. He was not attractive. He looked old and scary—nothing like us.

Walking inside, I could feel my throat tighten. Suddenly, it felt like I was paralyzed. My sister took the lead. She said hello. We sat down, and everyone began to talk. I just sat there and listened. I had initiated the meeting, but I wasn't speaking. Thank God Stacy was there to keep the conversation going. I couldn't wait to leave. The only person I enjoyed talking to was his son. He seemed more like us, while Bill and his wife didn't seem like people I wanted to know. I felt bad about that, but I couldn't help it. The dinner dragged on, and I managed to speak up occasionally, but I certainly wasn't myself. It felt like I had regressed to the way I was when I was a child. When it was time to go, we said goodbye, left things open to meet again, but of course we never did. A few years later, Bill died.

If my sister hadn't been there, I would have backed out. I never would have had the courage to get in the car and make the drive, never mind walk into that restaurant. I am so grateful to her for making the trip with me. The reason that moment was so big in my own personal growth was that I saw how my fears were not warranted. The dinner was awkward, but it was nothing like what I had built up in my head. Facing my fear and taking that step to walk directly toward it gave me more confidence for the next set of challenges that I would encounter. For a long time, I would draw strength from that experience.

CHAPTER 24

BUT FIRST, BABY STEPS

As I've mentioned, I was not always a confident person. I knew I was capable, but I let fear hold me back, and because of that, I suffered early in my professional career.

When I first started working as a salesperson in radio back in Worcester, I never felt confident enough to share my ideas in meetings. That seems so easy to do, but for years, I was afraid of what other people would say. It limited my advancement, and I knew it. I was sick of listening to people with lackluster ideas speak up when I knew my ideas were better. I had to face that fear monster head-on.

First, I made a promise to myself that I would contribute at least one idea in every meeting. That was it. The first time I raised my hand to contribute, I was petrified. I have no idea what I thought was going to happen, but the fear paralyzed me. I didn't give in. I shared my idea, and the meeting went on. The people didn't erupt with applause, but they didn't kick me out or shut me down either. It was just kind of normal. That inspired me to do it again in the next meeting. Pretty soon, it became my normal practice, and each meeting I would contribute a minimum of one idea. Then it became two ideas. Then it became speaking up when I disagreed. Quite soon, I didn't have to make a conscious effort to speak up. It had become natural. That one small step allowed me to find my voice at work and in meetings. I slowly began to get more respect and became better known among coworkers. Why didn't I do this sooner?

That was another early step that started me down the path to overcoming fear. It was an example that I could use to remind myself that if I pushed through the fear, I would have the opportunity to grow. Finding the confidence to speak in meetings helped me to realize that there were other areas in my life where I held back because of fear. For example, I've come up with about five different ideas for various apps over the years. One was an idea to build an app that allowed everyone to connect based on location. I did my research and learned that there wasn't anything like it. I spoke with a developer, but once I realized that I needed to raise capital to build the app, I gave up. I gave up on all the app ideas. I had a million reasons why I couldn't do it, but I didn't come up with a single reason why I should do it. I had bought into the theory that I was lucky to have a job and was getting by while caring for my son, so I should be grateful for what I had. I wrote about my ideas in my journal, but I never took action. I always made some excuse, but the real reason was fear. That had to change.

At the end of every year, I'd force myself to map out what it was I wanted for myself the following year. It included goals for work, fitness, and my relationships with my fiancé and son. Every year, there was always a spot on that list dedicated to starting my own business. That was a dream I had for two decades. I had a bunch of ideas on how I could help women realize their potential and build confidence. One extension of that brand was a clothing line based on the same initiative, but the problem was that I never did anything about it. One of my goals for 2017 was to never let fear be the reason why I didn't take the next step toward doing something I wanted to do. It was time for me to stop writing about my brand and time for me to make it happen. That was the moment I decided to move beyond idea and into execution.

I was terrified. I had never worked in the clothing industry, but I did know someone on the inside. Sort of. Oscar was someone I knew from the gym and through other mutual friends, but he was also the CEO of Perry Ellis—a huge job at a massive company. Obviously, I was afraid to reach out to him, but I had to keep that promise to myself. I didn't want to let fear hold me back from doing what I wanted to do for another whole year, so I sent him an email. I asked if there was a time that I could meet with him in the office to pitch him an idea. Good, right? Well, I never heard back. Crickets.

When I was younger, not hearing back from someone felt like a death sentence. *They must hate me. They must be laughing with their fabulous friends about my terrible email.* Luckily, after years of being in sales, I've learned that there are countless reasons why someone might not respond to your email. It could have wound up in his spam folder. Maybe he saw it for a second before boarding a plane and forgot about it when he landed because he was distracted by the one hundred new emails he received since then. Maybe there was an emergency. It's so easy for people to get caught up in their own lives. It really isn't always about you. Bottom line: You need to reach out again.

I had to reach out to Oscar a few more times, but eventually I got a response. He said that he would love to have me in the office so he could hear my idea. BOOM! Taking that first step and overcoming fear set that new opportunity in motion. That feeling of putting myself first and seeing it through was like nothing else I ever experienced. I was so proud of what I'd accomplished. None of my initial fears turned out to be true. Fear is a liar. It once controlled me, but now I control it. I now use fear as a motivator to get me where I am meant to go. The only regret I have is that I let fear control me for so long.

Start overcoming your fears with small baby steps, and before you know it, you will be making leaps and bounds without thinking twice.

CHAPTER 25

FLIP THE SCRIPT

When I made the social media post about losing my job, a lot of people reached out to me. One of those people was Froggy from *The Elvis Duran Show* asking how he could help. I asked him if he could get me on the show, and shockingly, he did.

For those who don't know, Elvis Duran is one of the largest celebrity talents in radio and has more than ten million listeners. I find him to be uplifting and encouraging for people in all walks of life. He also plays a significant role in promoting charities and helping those in need. His show typically focuses on pop culture, so I was a little unsure of how I would fit in. I sent the producer Nate as much material as I could on who I was, what I stood for, and how I wanted to use my brand to help others build confidence and overcome adversity. However, I had no idea what I was going to talk about on air, and that made me terrified.

Whenever I had to do something new, I used to reach out to somebody who had done it before to get some tips or tricks, but I decided to do this on my own. I wanted to stand strong and go on air just being me. It had taken me years to get to that point, but it still didn't ease my mind. I promised that I wasn't going to put any pressure on myself. I was just going to go on the show and try to have a nice conversation.

That worked for a couple days, but as the trip got closer, panic began to creep into the back of my mind. On the day I flew to New York, I could hear that fear monster knocking on the door. *What if I don't sound good or I make a mistake? What if Elvis doesn't like me and we got into an argument? What if I completely blow it and am exposed as a fraud?* That underlying fear has a way of rearing its ugly head at the most crucial times, but it's completely normal. I've learned to flip those questions on their head—take those negative questions and make them positive ones. *What if Elvis loves me? What if I do a fantastic job? What if I am completely exposed as a shining star?* When I flip the questions, I can visualize myself succeeding, and that helps manifest my vision for what I want for my future. Now I could picture the show going well. I saw myself laughing with Elvis and his team while having fun just being me. That took the pressure off.

It didn't help that my friends decided to chime in with

their thoughts. "What if you get asked to be a regular on the show?" "What if you get a big break from someone listening?" I knew my friends meant that in the most positive way, but it gave me lofty expectations, and that stressed me out. I've learned that when you feel good and are not under pressure, it comes across and impacts people in a positive way. Unfortunately, the opposite is true as well. When you're stressed and feeling negative, that comes across, too. That's why I always try to come up with little tricks to get myself in a positive mindset. Before going on the show, I immediately brought myself back down to earth by saying that it would be worth it if I could reach and inspire just one person. When speaking to an audience of ten million, I felt confident that I could reach one person. That was a quick boost to my confidence.

I landed in New York the night before the interview. I had to wake up at 5:00 a.m. on the day of the show and got very little sleep. I was told to be camera-ready, so I arranged to have someone do my hair and my makeup before the show. I had never met either person, and that stressed me out. My hair and makeup didn't turn out exactly the way I would have liked, but I was fine to do the show. I put on my black pencil skirt suit; it feels like superhero attire for me. I immediately felt a spike in my power and self-confidence. Looking at myself in the mirror when wearing that suit reminded me of how much I had overcome and how proud I was to be trying something new. I was still nervous, but I found comfort in my previous victories. If speaking up during a meeting didn't kill me years earlier, going on a radio show wouldn't either. I knew that I had been there before and had gotten through it.

I arrived at the studio early and was thrilled and excited to see that the show had put my name all over the green room, but I still hadn't spoken to anyone about what we were going to discuss. Can you imagine going onto a radio show that reaches ten million listeners and not knowing the topic of the interview? In the past, I would memorize everything I wanted to say and plan a solid strategy because I wasn't confident in myself. I've since learned that when I take the mask off and be myself, I'm at my best. That was my secret for reaching others, and I knew I could do that.

A few minutes before I went on air, Nate tracked me down in the green room and asked if there was anything I didn't want to talk about. I told him that I was open to discussing anything. That was it. I was on!

Elvis was prepared and started the segment off by talking about an award I had recently won. I was definitely nervous during the first few minutes of the interview, but as we talked and started laughing, everything became easy and fun. Things went so much better than I'd anticipated. I saw the phone lines light up like a Christmas tree after talking about overcoming a termination. That was a huge win! Elvis Duran was exactly what I'd expected. He was kind, thoughtful, sincere, and truly special. His team was welcoming and supportive. Their ease put me at ease. It was so refreshing to get to spend time with people who were doing what they loved. I could actually feel it. I had just been fired, so witnessing this reinforced the idea that finding a career I was passionate about was definitely possible.

The conversation shifted to overcoming fears, and I talked about being so nervous before going on air. Elvis said, "I believe that men don't think things through, whereas women think things through so much that they get to a place where they have considered everything that can potentially go wrong, and that leaves them feeling afraid. A man just goes and does it." During the show, we received so many encouraging calls and posts on social media telling me how inspiring the show was. Elvis even asked me to come back on the show when I finished my book, which was a major surprise.

At the end of the interview, Elvis also told me, "There is a fine line between fear and excitement." He was right. I was definitely scared that things wouldn't go well, but once I got through that, the experience was exhilarating. It was a rush and it was fun—something I never would have felt had I let fear get the best of me. That's why I challenge myself daily to plow through the fear so I can get to the excitement that lies on the other side. It works every time I try it, and it will work for you, too.

CHAPTER 26

CURRENTLY CHANNELING WONDER WOMAN

I felt comfortable on *The Elvis Duran Show* because I was talking about something I knew. I was in my wheelhouse, and in those moments, I feel unstoppable. It's so much easier to be confident in situations when you know what you're talking about, but what happens when you find yourself outside of your wheelhouse? How do you call on confidence in those situations?

On International Women's Day in 2017, I was asked to appear on i24NEWS with host Michelle Makori. At that point, I was still at my old job, but I had already launched my own personal brand aimed at empowering women and helping others get ahead. That was a passion project for me. After two decades spent mentoring others at work, I learned that most people struggled with the same challenges and obstacles. By launching my website and my brand, I could expand my reach far beyond the one-on-one counseling that limited my potential impact. Going on shows such as Elvis Duran and i24, I was able to shine a light on women's issues. I wanted to give people a real take on what was happening in the work place and how it affected real women.

The big difference was that this was a live international news show. I was excited for the opportunity and the chance to do something new, but it was most definitely out of my comfort zone. I did some research on topics that I thought Michelle might bring up and decided that I was as ready as I was ever going to be to appear on the program, but I was still scared. On the drive through New York City to the studio in Times Square, fear was starting to take over. I had to stop and regroup. Fear has the power to cripple you and prevent you from taking action. It can also throw you off your game so you don't perform at your best.

I needed to think fast. Who do I know that is able to steamroll anyone during an interview? Immediately, Donald Trump came to mind. Love him or hate him, I think we can all agree that fear doesn't faze Trump. What I've noticed about Trump is that he doesn't seem to care if he's right or wrong. He just answers with his gut and moves forward with total confidence. I've seen journalists ask him questions that he clearly doesn't know the answer to, but he simply pivots and answers the question that he wants to answer. *That's it! That's what I'm going to do. If he can do it, why can't I?* If the host asked me a question about international economics or another topic I knew nothing about, I would pivot and answer a question that I did know the answer to. This may not always be the best solution, but at that point in time, it was good enough to quell my fear and get me back to feeling confident. Beyoncé channels her alter ego Sasha Fierce when she takes the stage, and she comes off looking like one of the most confident women in the world. For my interview, I was going to channel my inner Donald Trump if I needed to.

I arrived at the studio and had a great interaction with the woman who did my hair and makeup. I was then miked up, brought out to the set, and seated next to Michelle. I was given an ear microphone, which was a new experience for me at that point. The first thing I noticed was that Michelle was very cold and British. When she asked, I told her that I was looking to talk about why women didn't go to work on International Women's Day and the bronze fearless statue that had been recently unveiled. Next thing I knew, we were live, and she was reading off the teleprompter. There I was, sitting in a studio atop Times Square appearing on a live international news show. That was big!

Michelle came at me aggressively on why I went to work

that day. That was easy for me to address. It set the tone and put me in my comfort zone. Things were going well, and then she asked me what the gender pay gap was outside of the United States. For those who know me, I've been outside the United States only a handful of times, so that was not a question I had an answer for. That was my moment. It was time to channel Donald. I did what he would do. I pivoted. "Great question. However, the real question here is why do companies not self-audit and share their findings? Why don't women ask their companies to be transparent?"

Boom! It worked!

The segment wrapped, and everyone thanked me. The producer came running out to tell me how amazing I was. My makeup artist friend was clapping. I left the studio and headed to meet a friend for sushi. I remember thinking how small New York City seemed at that time. I felt like I could do anything. I was feeling that same excitement Elvis Duran spoke of, and to think that I would have missed that rush had I given in to the fear I felt on the ride over to the studio.

If you find yourself nervous, scared, or out of your element, try channeling a different persona. Picture yourself handling a situation just like that person would handle it. Watch the way it unfolds with ease. When you visualize yourself behaving the way you want to behave and having the strength and courage to tackle any obstacle, it better allows you to perform when the moment occurs and the pressure is on because you've been there before. The next time you find yourself in an uncomfortable or unfamiliar situation, who will you channel?

CHAPTER 27

THE FRAUD MINDSET

"What does it take for a woman to get ahead? How did you get to where you are in business?" These are questions I'm asked all the time, and they are easy for me to answer. It takes hard work. You have to push and not back down. You have to be a pit bull at times.

I said that once to a coworker, and she told me, "That's hard to do because most women don't want to appear bitchy." That conversation struck a chord with me. That woman was bright, beautiful, talented, and interested in advancing. I couldn't predict what level she could rise to, but I did know that her talent WOULD NOT hold her back. She had everything it took to get ahead. The only limitation was inside herself, and addressing it was the first step in overcoming the fraud mindset.

LOOSEN YOUR OWN LEASH

That woman's decision to not want to appear "bitchy" would be her own personal leash. We all have a leash, and those leashes are not always in plain sight, but the more aware we are of the fraud mindset, the easier those leashes are to spot and remove.

YOU ARE NOT A FRAUD

A friend of mine was recently promoted but confided in me that because she didn't have much experience in her field that she felt like a fraud. She went so far as to tell her husband that she had a plan B lined up in case she was told that she wasn't qualified for the job. I've felt that same way at times, and many women I know have felt like frauds, too, but I have yet to see it in a man. In fact, the men I work with feel the opposite way. Whenever I've heard a man talk about wanting to advance without any prior experience, he will use his prior success as evidence that he will succeed in his new role. He doesn't consider it a big leap. It's a natural progression on his path to future success. Why don't we think like that?

YOUR SECRET IS OUT

Women don't always see those same challenges as a natural progression. Instead, they feel afraid of being "found out." Found out that they are not perfect. Found out that they have commitments at home to their families. Found out that they simply don't have all the answers. Meanwhile, I meet with men on my team who can't wait to share with me how they leave work early to coach their kid's team. Some go so far as to say that their coaching duties actually benefit the company because their leadership qualities are refined on the field and applied in the workplace. Believe it or not, nobody expects us to be perfect. We all have responsibilities at home. No need to hide that or make excuses.

PUT THINGS IN PERSPECTIVE

The way we choose to approach life is influenced heavily by the lens through which we view the world. By making a definitive decision to no longer accept the idea that we are frauds and choosing to replace that lens and look through one that allows us to celebrate our unique and more positive qualities is a major step in freeing ourselves from that leash. Yes, I have felt like a fraud at different times throughout my career. The difference with me is that I've been able to identify that behavior and change it, and so can you. Perspective is everything, and something as simple as learning how others view you is a good way to help change your perception. Most members of the opposite sex would never consider themselves frauds, so you shouldn't either.

LET US BE FRAUDS NO MORE

This is my new mantra. As women, let us embrace a refreshing new perspective. Don't be afraid to sprinkle in a little testosterone here and there. Let us celebrate what is unique about us and what makes us worthy of the opportunity in the first place. We rule the roost with no qualms. We learn as we go. We make executive decisions that are steadfast. Nobody knows everything. So let's see ourselves for what we are: talented people stretching ourselves to grow, definitely not fraudulent.

PART 5

. . . .

FINDING
YOUR VOICE

CHAPTER 28

JUST ASK

In order to get what you want, sometimes all you have to do is ask. That's it. Some situations require a little bit of finesse, but it all comes down to how you ask.

Recently, I was at a Dolphins game and my girlfriend wanted to get a plastic cup for her husband, but plastic cups are apparently held hostage at certain stadiums. We were at one of those stadiums because she asked nicely and was still denied a cup. She came to me and asked that I "work my magic." That made me laugh. Working my magic meant that I would go up to the counter and convince someone to give me a cup. Whenever you find yourself in a situation where it's difficult to ask for what you want, try to remember these ten basic rules.

1. HAVE COURAGE

You will only ever get what you have the courage to ask for. This is true in the stadium as it is in life. So why not ask for what you want? If you don't, someone else will, and you'll be bummed out that they got that plastic cup meant for you.

2. STAY CONFIDENT

Get your mind right before you act. Sometimes that's channeling Beyoncé's Sasha Fierce. I convince myself that nothing will knock me down. I'm on point. I've got this. Do whatever you have to do to get your mind right. Listen to music that fires you up. Think of a time you achieved something beyond your dreams. Grab onto that feeling, and use it as motivation that this can work, too.

3. SMILE

Never underestimate the power of a friendly smile. When you approach a stranger with a big smile, it's hard not to smile back. You've also opened the door for a conversation.

4. CONSIDER YOUR APPROACH

When you walk up to someone you don't know, you have to be friendly and authentic. For me, that means being upbeat and optimistic. For you, it might mean cracking jokes or giving a compliment. Be yourself, put your best foot forward, and make a quick connection.

5. GIVE OFF A GOOD VIBE

The vibe you put out is usually the vibe you will get back in return. When you stand tall, smile, and are open to meeting others, you are more likely to get that same attitude back in return. Make it clear that you are there to be positive and are asking for help.

6. PREPARE YOURSELF TO BE UNCOMFORTABLE

There is that brief period after you ask for what you want when you have to wait for the response. That is when things can get uncomfortable. It's so easy to walk away or doubt yourself. Power through. Smile and don't say anything. Let things play out before you respond. S/he who speaks first after the ask loses.

7. BE RELENTLESS

Relentlessness doesn't have to be a negative. Once someone answers with a reason why s/he can't give me what I want, I say something like, "I know you can do this. Come on, I'm sure there is a way we can make this happen." Often, people are so surprised by this that they quickly give you what you asked for. You just want to make sure that you remain positive and friendly the entire time.

8. DON'T ACCEPT "NO"

If you have truly tried everything and you keep getting turned down, then you need to kick it up to the next level. I would suggest saying, "I know that you can't make this happen, but is there someone who can? Is your boss able to do this? Is he or she here?"

9. BE READY TO PIVOT

Conversations can take a turn at any moment. You need to be ready to laugh or ultimately meet with a manager who might be annoyed you called them over. Be ready for anything, and try to have fun with it.

10. PRACTICE MAKES PERFECT

If you practice these steps over time, you will become an Ask Ninja. You will become the person your friends turn to when they need plastic cups during a football game. You have nothing to lose. The most important thing to remember is that you didn't have the cup when you started, so it's not the end of the world if you don't get it. Now, just be careful what you ask for.

CHAPTER 29

STAND YOUR GROUND

Ten years ago, I gave my birth to my son. I underwent a C-section, so when I returned home from the hospital, I was sore and exhausted. Those first few days as a new mother were terrifying. I was suddenly responsible for a tiny life but had no idea how to make sure that little guy thrived. I didn't realize how much tougher things were about to get.

Ten days after giving birth, I received a call from my then CEO who asked me to fly to his alma mater and give a speech to the students. *Wait. Did he really just ask me that?* I was in shock. Still suffering through issues stemming from my C-section, the last thing I wanted to do was hop on a plane and leave my brand-new baby behind to give a speech. The right thing for me to have done would have been to decline and come back to work when I was healthy, but that was a very sad time for me. I had low self-esteem, so I didn't have the confidence to say, "I just had a baby ten days ago. There is no way I can make a flight right now. I'm sure there is someone else in a better position who can make this trip and present to the students." I didn't even attempt to say no. Like a zombie, I just agreed.

If you Google my name, you can probably find the video of me presenting to that group of students in North Carolina. I look terrible. I hadn't slept. I was in pain and pumping in the bathroom before my speech. I was still wearing maternity clothes. That was a low moment for me. Agreeing to do the speech only made me more insecure and frustrated. It felt like the world was taking me places that I didn't want to go. Life was hard, but I didn't see the role that I played in it. I didn't see how my behavior and lack of boundaries led to that point. I never considered standing up for myself or putting my needs first. Hindsight is twenty-twenty, but that was a learning experience. It made me realize that we are responsible for our own path. Our decisions either help us build confidence or chip away at it.

Things have changed, and even though it was very difficult at first, it has gotten much easier with practice. I no longer have to deliberately remind myself to speak up. It has become second nature. Finding my voice means speaking up when I want to and not looking away when I'm annoyed or upset. Finding my voice means putting my needs first. Finding my voice empowers me, and people respond to that. Finding my voice has changed my life. Conversely, I have witnessed friends over the years stifle their voice and not use it. Those same women are often frustrated and discouraged and full of resentment. One of them even shared with me that she isn't feeling well physically, and she thinks it has something to do with holding her voice inside. Nothing in life is worth feeling resentful and sick over. The sooner you speak up, the easier it gets.

Prior to Hurricane Irma, my old boss, Jon, offered to let me and my fiancé use the private plane that he shares with a group of people. He gave us an amazing discount. At the last minute, he received a call from another friend who wanted to get his mom on board the plane and out of the storm's path. Jon sent me a text, asking if it would be OK and letting me know that his friend would be happy to pay his mom's way for a seat. We were happy to do it and, frankly, were happy to share the cost with someone else.

A few months later, I received an email from Jon's controller. It was an invoice for $10,800. My jaw dropped. Clearly, we were being charged for the entire flight. Had that occurred when I was younger, I would have swallowed the expense out of fear of speaking up and then stewed about it privately on my own time. Luckily, I had found my voice, so I simply shot back an email to the controller explaining the situation. I took a screenshot of the original arrangement I made with Jon, and we ended up paying for what we'd initially agreed. Simple. No fighting. No argument needed. Stand your ground and speak your mind.

These situations pop up in everyday life all the time. I was in spin class recently being taught by Ashli who was one of my favorite instructors. The instructors have a no-cell-phone policy in class because the workout room is typically dark and the vibe of the class gets thrown off when someone's phone suddenly rings or lights up. Countless times I've heard instructors speak about the importance of everyone leaving their phones outside of class. It means a lot to them, so if you have respect for the teacher, you don't bring your phone into class. Pretty simple, right? Well, last week in Ashli's class I saw a woman on her phone. Ashli got on the mic to ask those who needed to use their phones to leave the class. The workout continued, but the woman completely ignored the warning. Ashli had to get back on the mic and announce the same thing, but the woman remained on her phone. She was either ignorant or felt that she was above the rules. For a split second, I felt bad for Ashli, but then I saw her jump off her spin bike and confront the woman. "I've asked you nicely twice. Now I'm taking your phone, and you're leaving my class."

Ashli owned her voice, and I was so overwhelmingly proud of her. Her actions resonated with me. She decided not to complain about the woman who ignored the rules. Instead, she empowered herself by standing up and speaking her truth even though there was no guarantee that it would be met with a positive reaction. Apparently, I wasn't the only one who felt that way because the class erupted in applause. Shouldn't this be the way things go? They can be. By this point, you know the drill. If you aren't one of these people who stand up for yourself and speak your mind, start small. Chart your progress, and use those minor victories to inspire big change over time.

CHAPTER 30

FIVE PHRASES I FIRED

Finding your voice is about learning how and when to speak up, but it's also about learning when and what not to say. That was another lesson I learned the hard way. Here is a list of words and phrases that I have cut out of my vocabulary to empower myself.

1. YES

Whenever asked to do anything at work, my answer would always be "Yes" or "No problem." It didn't matter if I had the time or ability to complete the task because I feared it would leave a negative impression if I declined. I developed a mindset where I would take on the added responsibility when nobody else would. I didn't realize it at the time, but I was setting a dangerous precedent because people will treat you the way that you allow them to. Once I was able to identify that behavior, I made it a point not to be a dumping ground for tasks that nobody else wanted to do. Today, I consider my own priorities before I accept any new tasks. I am more mindful of my time and how extra responsibility will affect me. Even if my manager acknowledges the added burden, I make sure to have a conversation with that person. I ask questions and try to identify the best solution for all of us. If you find yourself with free time on your hands, it's a great idea to volunteer for a project, but if you're accepting added work only out of fear, then you need to work on your self-confidence first. This is true in our personal lives as well. If you are the one always saying yes to doing the errands, laundry, and not having a say in plans, it will leave you feeling less than important.

2. THIS ISN'T FAIR

If "Yes" is the cause, then "This isn't fair" is the effect. Not speaking up and not creating boundaries at work can lead to your becoming overwhelmed with too much responsibility or being taken advantage of. This inevitably leads to frustration. When I used to get upset that others didn't take on the same workload and challenges that I did, I would often complain to my boss. I may have been right, but what I didn't realize at the time was that I also had the power to change things. By creating boundaries and respecting my time and commitments, I was able to more accurately assess what I could realistically take on. This forced management to lean on others at times when they would typically turn to me. Remember that we can change how people treat us by changing how we treat ourselves.

3. I DON'T AGREE, BUT I WILL MAKE IT WORK

When I began working for a kind person after years of working for unpleasant employers, I found myself wanting to keep him happy. That often meant doing whatever he said. Even if I had a better solution, I often kept my mouth shut and took the path of least resistance. One day, I realized that by keeping my mouth shut not only was I hurting myself, but in some cases, I was also hurting the company. Keeping others happy at work was never in my job description, so I made the decision to respectfully make my opinion known when I disagreed. I now spend time trying to convince others why my idea will work. When I can't successfully convince management to change their decision, I make my disagreement known so it's on record that I did everything in my power to improve the situation. This also forces the person in question to truly consider your position, and it might leave them thinking twice about moving forward their way. When you know you have the best solution, speak from a place of strength. Try saying this: "I don't agree, but luckily I have another solution."

4. I FEEL

Beginning a statement by saying "I feel" immediately takes the power away from you by making the statement more emotional than factual. For example, would it be stronger to say, "I feel that choosing to pass on this candidate is the right decision," or "Passing on this candidate is the right decision"? Obviously, it's the second statement. If you want to be taken seriously at work and have your voice heard, then drop "I feel" from your vocabulary.

5. LIKE

This one was a difficult habit to break. Do you say a word so often that you don't even realize you're saying it? That's how I was with the word *like*. Thankfully, I had a few friends let me know in private that using the word *like* made me sound uneducated. Even they noticed how I was using the word to fill in the gaps during conversations. Since learning this, I have nixed the word from my vocabulary, and I try to help others do the same. It's hard enough when you're perceived a certain way because of your exterior; couple that with using words that don't add value and you're making things tougher than they need to be. Eighty-six the *like*.

CHAPTER 31

COMMAND RESPECT

I recently ran a contest on my Instagram feed giving away a free coaching session so I could help others who might be struggling with work or just life in general. Like any other time in my life, when I work to help others I get a boost.

I couldn't pick just one winner, so I decided to choose six winners. That meant scheduling six hours of coaching in one week. That was six hours that I really didn't have, but I found a way to make time for them. While I was a little annoyed with myself when the scheduled time neared, after my calls I felt beyond invigorated. I also noticed an obvious thread that seemed to weave all of the calls together. Women typically struggle with similar things regardless of where they're from, what they do, or where they are in their lives. No matter which call I was on, each woman felt a lack of respect at work and felt they were treated in a way they didn't deserve.

My first call was with a young professional Latina who happened to live in Miami. Her excitement and energy were contagious. She was beyond prepared to make the best of her hour. She had a list of questions and some examples of situations that she wanted help with. We discussed how to become a stronger public speaker. I told her how to connect with her audience by leading with a relatable story and how to position herself as an expert. I instructed her to go to www.helpareporter.com and answer media inquiries so she could begin developing her own PR campaign. Pretty soon, we got to the question that I was asked on every single one of those calls: "How do I get people at work to respect me?" When conducting training sessions during her job, the woman felt like she was constantly challenged and made to feel less than. "I don't know what to do, and I end up apologizing even though I know that I'm right."

Hearing that young and very smart woman's problem resonated with me. I was so happy that we were connecting because I had been in her shoes and could share my experiences. It's never easy being a woman in a meeting and being challenged by a more senior male. Just like it's never easy when your boss won't give you an answer on why you haven't been approved for a raise when it is clear you're doing a great job and other employees are getting a raise. There are so many times in our work life, and even in our personal life, when we know we aren't getting the respect or treatment we deserve but have no idea what steps must be taken to change it. After fourteen years in corporate America, and a few years in the C-suite, I have encountered my share of challenges from others in the workplace and figured out tactics and tools that allowed me to leapfrog right over them.

First, if someone is disrespecting you or treating you badly, you need to deal with it head-on. Like anything else, how you allow others to treat you is how they will treat you. Others will see that and follow suit. It is critical to nip poor behavior in the bud. The longer it goes on, the more challenging it becomes to change, but it's possible. As with anything, it's a process.

If you aren't able to address the issue immediately, it's important to leave the situation and write it down on a piece of paper. Jot down what that person said to you when s/he behaved in a manner that wasn't warranted. *"Why should we do these things you're outlining in this presentation? They sound like more work, and frankly, we are too busy. Are you done yet?"* Then write down what you WANT to say the next time you are in that situation. Keep it strong, professional, clear, and direct. *"As the director of HR, it is my job to protect the company and you. Clearly, we haven't broken through this yet, so the real question is, what do you need to do in order to process this and understand it so we are not here longer than we need to be?"* Now memorize it.

The act of practicing and memorizing what you want to say will help set you up for future success.

Next, it's critical that you visualize yourself having that successful conversation where you stand up for yourself in the next meeting. That was when the young woman I was working with started laughing. When I asked her why, she said it was because when she imagines herself saying that, she literally sees herself breaking down with nervous laughter. That made one thing clear to me: she needed to practice visualization a lot more. The more you visualize yourself doing something and visualize the desired outcome, the more you prepare yourself for success in a future situation. If it takes days of your visualizing yourself delivering your line in a calm and confident manner, then that is what you need to do. Practice. If you truly believe it in your mind, then it is not only possible, but it is also probable.

Now that you know what you're going to say and visualized yourself doing it successfully many times, climb into your superhero gear before your next meeting. Literally, you want to wear that outfit that screams confidence to you. For me, that is my power suit. It makes me feel unstoppable. We know that the clothes we choose affect how others think of us, but it also affects our own thoughts about ourselves. Find your superhero gear and wear it with the confidence of Wonder Woman. Channeling your inner superhero will help you to own that power and stand with confidence when you walk into the room. So much of what we do comes through in how we stand. Keep your shoulders back and head up. No need to fidget. Lock eyes with others. That's key in ensuring they treat you with respect. Backing down is not an option now that we're in our Wonder Woman gear. You will now be ready. Embrace this newfound power you created.

This may sound like a lot of work, and honestly, it is. Being successful takes work, and it doesn't happen by accident. It takes preparation, which is why confidence isn't given; it is learned. If success was easy, everyone would have it.

CHAPTER 32

SPEAKING UP 101

Tucker was a vendor based out of New York City with whom I worked. After working together for a couple of years, he became my mentor without my even realizing it. I knew that he was in the office very early every morning, so if I wanted to get things accomplished with him, I would need to call him at 7:30 a.m. before everyone else got into the office. Whenever we spoke, he always gave me his full attention and offered to help any way he could. He also took a personal interest. He'd ask me about my goals and vision for the future. Tucker knew that I loved to help others, so one day he suggested that I get involved with charity to help fill a void that I wasn't able to fill in my job.

That conversation opened my eyes and helped me understand that just because I was great at my job and developed a strong reputation, it didn't mean that there wasn't more out there for me. Thanks to his guidance, I began the process of discovering my passion. What was my mission? How could something I love and was good at mesh with what the world needed while still allowing me to make money? Looking for answers to those questions has been a life-changing move.

Immediately after that conversation with Tucker, I joined City Year Miami, and they asked me to host their women's luncheon. That was years ago, back when I had a harder time saying no to things, so of course I was terrified, but because it was for charity, I knew that I had to make myself do it. Once I showed up at the event, I realized that I was surrounded by such amazing women who were all there to support one another. That sense of camaraderie put me at ease, so by the time I stepped on stage and up to the podium, I was no longer scared. I was excited. The positive reaffirming message I wrote on the bottom of my heels didn't hurt either. Each year that I hosted the luncheon, I would feel my excitement and confidence grow. Each year, there were more women with great feedback that made the work so fulfilling. I was exposed to a whole new world that I hadn't been a part of before. The more I embraced that superpower, the stronger I became. I was also growing my network and making new contacts, which resulted in more speaking engagements at bigger events. I am constantly reminded that putting your best foot forward in an arena that lets you utilize your superpowers will pay dividends down the road while creating a domino effect leading you toward success and positivity.

People approach me a lot for advice about public speaking. I, the same woman who was scared to speak up in meetings, am now not only giving other people advice on public speaking, but I also learned that public speaking was actually my superpower. Go figure. If I can do it, anyone can do it. No matter who you are, there are times in your life when you have to speak in public. If you are a student, you will need to present in front of your class. Maybe you're attending your best friend's wedding and you need to give a toast. You could also be so frustrated with your sorority, parent-teacher association, charity, or book club that you need to muster the strength to stand up and address the issues in front of the group. Those moments are terrifying for some, which is why public speaking is one of the most common fears people have today. It doesn't have to be terrifying. Here is a list of tips and tricks I picked up along the way.

1. START EACH SPEECH WITH A STORY

Pick a story that you don't have to read notes to tell—a real-life story. People enjoy listening to someone who is authentic and is giving them a glimpse into his or her own life. The best speeches I've given are ones when I spoke from the heart and talked about my own life struggles. That will keep the audience's attention. If you aren't looking at notes, you can make eye contact. When I get stuck or don't have an applicable story, I'll ask my friends, and they will often have a perfect example that I can use. The funny thing is that stories tend to be the part of the presentation that everyone remembers.

2. MEMORIZE YOUR NOTES

Not every single speech allows you to tell a personal story, but you want to apply the same principles. If you're forced to work off notes, memorize those notes so you don't have to bury your head and read while presenting. Not looking up and speaking freely can cause you to lose your audience. When working off a script, I like to highlight key words that I know will trigger my memory. That way, if I get lost, I can glance down at my paper and see the next topic. The notes become a safety net. Even when you aren't telling a personal story, find a way to approach the subject matter that allows you to speak from your heart. Put your own unique spin on it. That will make it more relatable.

3. GET THE AUDIENCE INVOLVED

This doesn't mean that you need to interview the audience or call someone out, but you can ask them big-picture questions such as, "Has anyone in this room ever felt they couldn't accomplish something but tried anyway?" Even if no one yells out, you've gotten everyone's attention and can continue by saying something like, "Well, that is me today, so bear with me while I'm up here." You could also plant someone in the audience, such as a friend or coworker, who answers that question a certain way. That makes the whole experience more interactive while also giving you a little break.

4. SHAKE UP THE AUDIENCE

Ask everyone to stand and stretch if you're the fourth speaker during a daylong meeting. Make a joke. "It's 3:00 p.m. on a Friday, so I'm sure that you're all just dying to hear what I have to say." It's also helpful to use people's first names when speaking. This can make the story more relatable while further engaging the audience.

5. USE A VISUAL AID

Presentations are not always for people you know and are often about some dry or boring topics. When that is the case, I find it useful to use a PowerPoint or Keynote presentation on the big screen. I will use basic images to help make a topic visual, but it's also there to remind me of where I need to go next with my speech. It's another way to avoid looking down to read my notes while also engaging the audience with visuals. This will help them retain the information after the presentation.

6. PRACTICE IS CRUCIAL

Some of the smartest and most talented people I know practice for weeks before making a presentation. If you're nervous about speaking and haven't practiced, you're setting yourself up for failure. You get out what you put in. Know your strengths and weaknesses so you know what you need to prepare. Keep detailed notes. Highlight those notes if needed. Practice by yourself. Practice in front of other people to see where you might trip up. This is a game changer because feedback from others is helpful. If you have friends and coworkers who have seen you speak before, ask for their feedback. I constantly ask people what they thought I could have done better and what they took away. That is a great way to gain insight into how others see you.

7. VIDEO IS YOUR FRIEND

I had been speaking at events for years before I ever saw myself on video. Part of me was just too nervous to see how I sounded and looked. I just assumed that I would hate what I saw. That was an epic mistake. When I was asked to put together a reel, I had to go back and beg people to dig up any video of old speeches, but nobody could find anything. Fortunately, one person did. I forced myself to watch it and found it to be surprisingly good. It's funny how we're always our toughest critics. By watching the video, I learned that I excelled while speaking freely, but I was not good at reading the video monitor. My new goal is to get video of every speaking engagement so I can build a great reel and learn from each event. Imagine how well you will know your tendencies and habits once you see what others see. You can even practice while video rolls. I promise it will not be as painful as you think.

8. YOU DON'T HAVE TO BE PERFECT

It's natural to want to be perfect, but how many presentations have you sat through without paying much attention to the speaker? The sad reality is that the audience is easily distracted. So many people are preoccupied by their phones or what's going on in their own lives. Most aren't even worried about you. When you shift your perspective and take this into account, it can alleviate some of the pressure. You don't have to be great. You often just have to be good enough.

9. DON'T RULE OUT HYPNOSIS

Hypnosis is a proven solution for people who are paralyzed by fear. I've seen it work on numerous people, and I have done it myself. The one caveat is that you have to be open-minded to it working and want it to work. Find a well-respected hypnotist who specializes in the field. Don't count this out. It really does work.

10. YOU ARE GOOD AT THIS

When in doubt, I pull out that same handy list of success stories that I always keep within arm's reach. I look back over the times that I received positive feedback from others, and it gives me an instant boost. On this list, I also cite five times when I was nervous and turned things around. Recently, I saved my 2017 year in review on my Instagram Stories Highlights. I love going back to watch it! Reminding yourself of your accomplishments and reflecting on them will give you strength. When in doubt, a little message on the bottom of your shoes doesn't hurt either. You can do all things!

PART 6

. . . .

TAKING ACTION

CHAPTER 33

GETTING STARTED

It's time to use what we've learned and make changes. This is never easy. Nobody can just flip a switch and suddenly become a different person. It takes work, but here are some things to keep in mind on the road ahead.

BALANCE IS BULLSHIT

A lot of woman would tell me that I needed to find my work-life balance. We all struggle with this, mainly because BALANCE DOES NOT EXIST when you are a wife, mother, or employee. There is no perfect harmonious balance. I've never seen it because it's not real. Unfortunately, we as women have all grown up in a society that puts emphasis on men succeeding in work. Men didn't have pressure to create a good home life. Parenting responsibility never fell on the shoulders of men the way it did on women. That has begun to change over the years, but it won't go away instantaneously. As women, we were not traditionally responsible for being the best employee, spouse, or breadwinner, but what happens when a woman is a single parent? Not only is she the sole breadwinner, but she also has to do it all because there is no spouse. Try telling a single mom about finding the perfect work-life balance. You don't have to be a single mother to feel that massive responsibility. I frequently hear from married women who tell me their husbands aren't pulling their weight. If you're feeling like that, the first thing you have to do is lighten up on yourself. You can't do it all. No one can. No one does. We have days when we're killing it at work and things are phenomenal at home, but then there are times when work is a disaster and we dread going home. If everything with your kids is going well, you can afford to work more or focus on yourself, but if those children are struggling, they are the ones who need your attention. Every one of you probably knows by now that things will not stay good forever, but that should reinforce the idea that they won't stay bad forever either. That's why balance is bullshit. Things change, and you have to be ready to ride the wave whether it goes up or it goes down.

WHAT'S IMPORTANT TO YOU?

As we grow, our priorities change, which is why it's important to check in with yourself from time to time. You constantly want to assess your situation and adjust your mindset accordingly. It's so easy to get wrapped up in our own goals and desires that other areas of our lives are neglected. If you have been single for years and never had the time to date, it might be time to make that a priority. You still want to create goals and work hard to accomplish them, but remember that success and happiness is a moving target. You have to keep readjusting and reevaluating so life doesn't pass you by.

NO ONE CAN DO THIS ALONE

If you try to take everything on alone, you are setting yourself up for failure. We all need help. Family, friends, coworkers, and your spouse—those people are your support system. It might surprise you to learn how many people will rise when you call. You'll never know if you don't ask. Don't suffer alone if you don't have to. I couldn't live without the support of my friends and family. Those are the people I call when I need to make sure that I'm setting a good example for my son. If I'm spending too much time at work and neglecting my family, I need those same people to keep me in line. Find your team. Tap them often and ask them for help. What do you have to lose? If you have a friend who won't help you in your time of need, how much of a friend is that person? Send them packing.

WHAT DOES SUCCESS LOOK LIKE?

So many people say that they want success without really thinking about what success specifically means to them. For some, success is the best job and the largest bank account. Work will always be a priority for those people. For some, it's having a happy family life that will be second to none. It's easy for those people not to get caught up in work or forget about their loved ones. The people who have a more difficult time defining success are those of us who want to excel at work and have a full family life. I try to make sure that I prioritize when needed. Unfortunately, I can't answer this question for you. It's different for everyone, but figure out what success looks like to you and prioritize your life accordingly. When you take a closer look and really examine your goals, you might be surprised by how much they have changed since you set them.

FIND YOUR PASSION

I have heard from women who say that they don't know what their passion is, but they are sure that they're not following it. What are you passionate about? What would you love to do if money wasn't an issue? For me, my passion is helping others who are struggling. It reminds me of who I am and where I've been. That helps make me more confident and proud of where I am today. Everyone has a different passion. Yours might be writing or painting or spending time with children. Once you identify that passion, find a way to weave it into your life. It doesn't have to be your career or main source of income. It can be a hobby or charity work. It can be something you do with your family on weekends. When you make your passion part of your life, it will make everything else in your life better.

BE PRESENT IN THE MOMENT

By being present in every moment, you will put more into that task and deliver a better result. When you're at work, focus on being the best you can be. If you take a day off to go on a field trip with your child, focus on where you are and not terrorize yourself over what you might be missing at work. Make the most of where you are today. When you're having a difficult day, don't envision where you hope to be two years from now when "things will be better." The time to plan for your future is when you're calm and not feeling unbalanced. We all feel down and inadequate at times. It is normal, but those are the times to do what makes you feel good. Spend time with your loved ones, meditate, or work out. Do whatever it takes. Don't avoid it or try to escape it. Embrace the moment, whatever it may be, and use it to your advantage.

DON'T PUT YOURSELF LAST

Want to increase the chance of failure? There is no better

way than putting yourself last, yet so many women do this to themselves. The better you take care of yourself, the better you can care for your family and the better you can do your job. Don't make excuses. Stand strong. If you know that working out will set your mind for the day and increase your productivity, make time to work out. If you feel better about yourself when you get your hair colored, make an appointment and don't feel bad about it. If you are not the best you, then you will be limited in what you can take on. You'd be surprised the positive impact this will have on those around you. When you feel better, you perform better. You have more energy to give your loved ones. Balance may be bullshit, but making yourself a priority cannot be. Don't make excuses when it comes to giving yourself exactly what you need.

TAKE VACATIONS

I used to think that people who took vacations were slackers. Wow, was I wrong. I've learned that the people who get away and detach themselves from work are the smart ones. They come back ready to engage. They feel invigorated and creative, while those who don't vacation often burn out and become resentful. Make time to be with your loved ones when you are detached and away from work. Make memories that you will never forget. Planning trips will give you and your family something to look forward to. It doesn't have to be a long or expensive trip.

The purpose is to spend time with the people who mean the most to you. Take time to explore what the world has to offer. If you don't stop and look around once in a while, you could miss it.

CHAPTER 34

YOUR VIBE ATTRACTS YOUR TRIBE

Growing up, I gravitated toward the kids who were suffering or struggling. I wanted to help them, but they were also the people who I felt the most comfortable around. I felt at home on the island of misfit toys. I didn't know it at the time, but I was insecure and scared of people knowing the real me. I was afraid other kids wouldn't like me or wouldn't think I was worthy of being their friend. Because I was so scared of opening up, I would remain on that island for years to come.

My father once asked me why I surrounded myself with people who I needed to help. He thought I should seek out people who would help me grow and who I wanted to be like instead of those I needed to save. I didn't understand or appreciate what he was saying at the time, but he was right. I didn't have friends whom I could turn to in order to lift me up. Most of my friends were pulling me down.

Luckily, I always played sports. Sports taught me a new sense of self-worth. Becoming part of a team allowed me to meet and surround myself with a new group of people who left me feeling energized. It took me years to realize that I could choose the people whom I associated with. I had the power to essentially hire and fire those I let into my inner circle. They don't teach you that in school, but getting rid of people pulling you down is like freeing yourself from an anchor chained to your body. Ever notice how the more exposed you are to negativity, the more it begins to rub off on you? I am a firm believer that you attract the same type of energy that you give off. Why would anyone want to attract negativity or bring that into their lives?

Old habits die hard. The funny thing about habits is that they become second nature. When this happens, we don't even realize we're engaging in self-destructive behavior. Even though I began to cut negative people out of my life when I was a kid, I didn't completely understand the concept, so as an adult, I still gravitated toward people who brought me down without even realizing it. One eye-opening experience occurred when I was a young mother. I had a friend named Jen whom I spent a lot of time with because we both had children the same age. Jen was an asset to me at a time when I was still finding my footing as a newly divorced mom without any family in Miami. I was able to spend time with her family and learn parenting skills. On the surface, the relationship seemed great.

Jen was the kind of girl who always knew what to do, where to go, and how to act. She never gained weight, drank too much, or spoke too loudly. She seemed perfect, but after spending time with her, I would leave feeling discouraged. I didn't notice it at first, but over time, I picked up on her disapproving looks and negative quips that would leave me feeling less than. I let those comments go, mainly because I didn't want them to be true. I didn't have a large circle of mom friends back then, and I was desperate to connect with people who had kids my son's age.

My girlfriend Vanessa finally told me that she didn't want to come around if I had Jen over my house. She explained to me that Jen's fake perfect image was a turnoff, and she didn't like how it made her feel. *That's it!* I felt exactly the same way, but Vanessa was able to articulate what I had been unable to realize on my own. I suddenly looked at Jen in a completely different light. She tried so hard to seem perfect that it became stressful to watch. She wasn't at ease, and when I became more confident and comfortable with myself, it made her seem more uncomfortable in her own skin, as if it were a threat to that seemingly perfect facade. It was not a healthy friendship.

It was around that same time when I was going through my divorce and at my lowest. I felt like a failure as a mother and was beating myself up something fierce. That only made my situation worse. Thank God I had Kristina to lean on. Now, Kristina was the complete opposite of Jen. She always lifted me up and let me know that I was not to blame. She would talk on the phone with me late into the night as I cried. I credit her with getting me through that negative funk. She reminded me to listen to my own voice so I could remember what happened and why I felt the way I did. It was because of her that I was able to see things from a different perspective and regain hope in my future.

As I became a stronger, more confident person, I began to distance myself from Jen. She was not an awful person, but she wasn't supportive, encouraging, or accepting either. Her behavior would rub off on me in a negative way. Eventually, I stopped spending time with Jen altogether, not because she did anything wrong, but because I no longer liked the way I felt when I was with her. More importantly, I didn't feel like Jen was a person I could count on. A part of me didn't completely trust her with my true feelings. Kristina, on the other hand, remains one of my best friends to this day. During Hurricane Irma, it was Kristina who took in me and my family during our time of need and let us stay at her house for more than a week.

Try to remember that the people bringing you down are

already below you. Don't take it personally. Haters typically hate you for one of three reasons: they see you as a threat, they hate themselves, or they want to be you. Address these haters head-on, or find ways to cut them out of your life. Don't give them power by humoring or indulging their attacks. Whom you surround yourself with is a choice, and if you aren't happy with your life, then you need to take action to change it. Cutting negative people out of your life will make room for the positive ones to find their way in.

CHAPTER 35

BECOMING THE HERO OF YOUR STORY

What do you do if the person bringing you down in your life is a member of your family?

There is no easy way to address that situation. I know from experience. It happened back when I was going through my divorce. When I broke the news to my parents, my mother freaked out. She didn't want me to get divorced, and every time we spoke about the situation, she tried to talk me out of it. I had spent a lot of time mulling that over, and I knew that it was the right decision for me and my son. It hurt me tremendously to listen to her tell me that I was wrong and that I should suck it up. I asked her to support me because it was early in the divorce process and I didn't want to start doubting myself. However, all of our conversations would end with her telling me not to get divorced. Those phone calls left me feeling terrible and had me second-guessing my own feelings. It compounded the problem.

I couldn't cut my mother out of my life, and I didn't want to, but the tension wasn't helpful and it wasn't healthy. I learned it was necessary for me to put up boundaries. When she called, we'd speak until the conversation turned to divorce. I politely told her that the conversation wasn't helpful and that I had to go. That was it. I didn't get upset and I didn't start a fight. She learned over time that I didn't want to listen to her badger me over why I should stay married. If we were going to talk, I either needed her to be supportive or for her to avoid the topic of divorce altogether. Challenges with loved ones are not simple, but they do teach you how to speak up for yourself. A similar situation developed with my mother after I was fired, but by that point, I was prepared. I had learned from my previous mistakes. I was vulnerable and needed to stay positive, so I let her know what I needed, and she respected that.

You have the right to create personal boundaries. Just because you haven't made certain boundaries clear in the past doesn't mean that you can't create them today. You need to take responsibility for how others treat you by letting them know when a line has been crossed. Not doing that and letting family members or those close to you cross those boundaries can lead to a lack of self-confidence and a lack of control over your life. Setting clear limits demonstrates to others that you deserve respect. You can't change others, but you can change yourself, and it's often the most empowering step you can take.

Teaching others how we want to be treated and protecting ourselves from family members is uncomfortable, but it can be done. Keep in mind that this doesn't have to be a big confrontation. In so many cases, the disagreement comes down to a simple misunderstanding. I used to think that standing up for myself meant digging in and preparing for a fight. Over the years, I realized that oftentimes you simply need to state your needs and ask for what you want. There are bullies out there and there are times when you will need to dig in, but most people aren't inherently bad people looking to hurt you. In some cases, the other person has no idea they're hurting your feelings if you don't tell them. Working hard to communicate with the people in your life can improve your relationships by avoiding potential misunderstandings.

This goes both ways. Nothing hammered this lesson home for me more than when I was the offender. It happened during my son's fourth birthday party. Things became chaotic and I needed help, so I started barking orders to my boyfriend at the time. When the craziness died down, he pulled me aside and let me know that it wasn't appropriate for me to order him around. He was right, and I completely agreed. Sometimes we need people to point out how we are behaving so we can correct it. That's why a calm conversation with the offender might yield surprising results.

Only you know what you need. As soon as you understand your value, others will, too. Listen to your inner voice and support yourself. Don't wait for someone else to save you. Fair maidens are rescued only in fairy tales. You have to be a participant in your own rescue, and you can be the hero of your own story. You deserve better!

CHAPTER 36

GO FOR IT

It's so easy to trick ourselves into thinking that the way things are now is the only way that they will ever be. I can tell you without a doubt that this is not true.

Years ago, a big media company pursued me, but I didn't want to meet with them because I had already made up my mind that they couldn't give me the flexibility I needed with my son and would insist that I move to New York City. I came to this conclusion before I'd even met with them to discuss the job.

My good friend Jon heard my reasoning for passing up that opportunity and pointed out how I wasn't in a position to decide what the company would or wouldn't be open to. Instead, he told me that I should think I am so valuable that they would give me the flexibility I desired. If they didn't, it would be their loss. I liked that. How could I not? Any situation is possible if we believe we can make it happen. Why not envision the way we want things to turn out and be open-minded about our own success? What do we have to lose?

Jon is married to a strong woman, and both of them see things clearly when it comes to self-value. They don't mince words and they expect the best. At the time of that conversation, I did not feel the same way. While his words sounded good and were exactly the way I wanted to think, I didn't truly believe that about myself. Looking back, it's clear to me now that I avoided the interview because I was scared of being rejected. There is no guarantee that the company would have catered to my needs or even hired me, but not going to that interview ensured that I didn't get the opportunity I wanted.

Over time, my perception shifted and my confidence grew. I now take a page out of Jon's book and keep an open mind when pursuing opportunities. While writing this today, I am currently in the process of pitching my own show. I have no idea if things will pan out for me, but at this point, the outcome is irrelevant because I've already reaped tremendous benefits just by putting myself out there, taking a chance, and seeing where it leads. That alone builds my confidence.

The journey started a year earlier when I realized that

I was never going to be able to respond individually to all the women who were contacting me about how to overcome adversity, build their own brand, and be taken seriously at work. I needed a new way of reaching that large group of people, so I came up with the idea to create a show where I would work with a different woman each week to help her address her specific challenges. Yoav was a producer who helped me develop the project. Together, we worked with a small team and put together a pitch reel. That cost money and the financial investment was risky, but I knew that if I didn't take a chance, I wasn't going to ever know if I could make my dream a reality.

I invested the money and shot the reel but realized that I had zero experience pitching a television show. I needed help, and I asked a ton of questions. Luckily, Yoav got his agent to set up meetings with Bravo and WE in New York. I was completely out of my element. I had no experience. If it all had happened a few years earlier, I would never have put myself in that position. However, things were different, and I decided to dive in. The worst that could happen was someone would pass, which meant that I lost my investment in the reel. That would be a small price to pay for knowing that I tried my best instead of not trying and wondering what could have been. Again, building confidence.

Our first meeting was with the VP of development, but

he ultimately passed on the show because he felt that it didn't have enough drama. His vision for the show wasn't the type of show I was looking to make, but that meeting broke the ice. Our next stop was Bravo, where we met with a person on the team but not the VP of development. The challenge with a meeting like this was that she could pass on the project, but she couldn't say yes without approval. I don't like these types of meetings. It's always better to pitch the decision makers directly because nobody will ever sell you or your material as good as you will. Knowing that I had to get a yes from that woman in order to meet with her boss made that meeting much tougher. The pitch was met with similar resistance. The meeting was cut short, and we were told that she would share the reel with her team and get back to us in a week. A week later, we heard back. The network passed, once again because the show didn't have enough high drama like the franchises that had been so successful for their network.

That was it. I didn't want to re-create the *Housewives* franchise, and neither company was sold on my concept. I was disappointed. I believed in my idea. I knew it was viable and I knew it would work. I just had to pitch more networks to find the place that felt the same way I did. The challenge was that I didn't have an agent and I didn't know whom to call to pitch the show to. I reached back out to Yoav to see if he could set up more meetings, but his schedule had changed and he wasn't going to be back in New York City for quite some time, so he wasn't able to set anything up.

There are so many times in life when we think that we've exhausted every option when in reality there is more that we can do. Now that I was back to square one with my project, I challenged myself to come up with some different ways to pitch my show. I let all of my friends know what I was trying to do. Suddenly, I received a call from Amanda, my friend in Boston. She knew a woman who worked with a production company that might be able to help. I immediately called that woman up, and she loved my idea. I sent her my reel, and she loved it. She connected me with Shaun who was working on some new shows. He loved it! Then...crickets. Weeks passed and I didn't hear back. I emailed and texted. Nothing. I needed to try something else.

I targeted people on LinkedIn who worked at major networks, and while many people accepted my connections, none responded to my query regarding my reel or offered to put me in touch with people who could help. More crickets. I was doing that for weeks when I finally heard back from Scot at NBC Universal. Scot seemed kind and made it clear that I should keep my expectations low but that he would try to get the reel out to the right people at NBC. A few weeks later, he contacted me to say that the show wasn't the right fit for them and that I should try TLC or another network. I thanked Scot for his help and continued looking for ways to get meetings with other networks.

A few weeks later, I received a note from Scot. He asked if I was OK with him sending my reel to E! I was excited and appreciative but, as advised, kept my expectations low. E! contacted me a week later. We set up a phone call with the VP of talent who liked the idea enough to ask me to come out to Los Angeles to meet with the executive team face-to-face. As I'm writing this now, this meeting has yet to happen, but I will gladly get on that plane and see where this adventure takes me. The experience so far has been invaluable because I've met so many people and learned so much about this industry that I never would've learned had I not taken that first step and been open to following the road wherever it was going to take me. An object in motion stays in motion, so get moving.

CHAPTER 37

USE YOUR SUPERPOWER AS A SPRINGBOARD

On International Women's Day 2016, it felt like we were bombarded with messaging that suggested women needed to unite and be heard. It inspired me to contribute and make a difference, even if just in my own inner circle. It suddenly dawned on me that I was a leader at my company and I wasn't doing anything to recognize the day or unite my team on a level beyond our day-to-day jobs. I felt like I was letting my female team down for not creating a community that allowed us to support one another.

I sent out an email to the couple hundred women in my division. I wanted them to get to know me on a more personal level and hoped that I could get to know them the same way. I shared some personal information and asked those who wanted to participate to respond with a message to the entire group.

The response was overwhelming. I received more than a hundred emails. Women were reaching out and looking to support one another. They wanted to know about both wins and losses. I learned so much about my coworkers. Some were married, others divorced. We created a community of support that ultimately left all of us feeling connected and united. It was spectacular. I felt so proud. I had sent some insights to my boss, and he was overjoyed, but it was short lived.

A few weeks later, I received word that our new CEO was not comfortable with the group and wanted me to shut it down. Sure enough, a few days later my boss called and gave me verbiage to use in the email. I felt deflated, defeated, and devastated. On the upside, I had been able to create some new relationships that I knew would not go away, but I was so hurt that we couldn't continue with all that positive momentum we had built up during the previous weeks.

Right when the group disbanded, I received an email from a coworker named Cindy. It was a cry for professional help. She was lost and unhappy and had no idea what to do about it. I called her immediately to see if I could help. After speaking with her for only a few minutes, it became clear that she was unfulfilled. Her passion was stifled. She hadn't realized her superpowers yet. Worse, she was down on herself and told me that she didn't think there was anything that she was good at and had no idea how to change her life for the better.

I could relate because I've felt like that before. You probably have, too. It's not uncommon, but it shocked me to hear Cindy speak about herself that way because that was not my opinion of her at all. Cindy had been on my team for a few years. From the beginning, I thought she was extremely talented, and so did the other people who worked with her. While on the phone, I told her that I had never met anyone who could write as eloquently as she could. I was not telling her what she wanted to hear. I really was in awe of how I could send her a scattered memo that she could turn into a beautiful work of art in minutes. That was her superpower.

As we spoke more, she told me that she assumed everyone wrote just as well as she did. She really didn't recognize her own talent. Technically, she was allowed to utilize her superpower in her job but confided in me that the work she was doing was not interesting to her. It's not that she didn't like her job, but rather, she didn't have any passion for the content she was writing and editing. What she wanted to do was work on more important and meaningful things that could help others. That was Cindy's breakthrough moment. After that phone call, she was able to find her passion and redirect her focus. She's now working on material that she is passionate about.

We all get down and feel lost at times. In today's competitive and demanding professional world, it's easy to lose sight of your passion, but sometimes the solutions to our problems are right under our nose. We simply need to take a step back to fine-tune our focus so it's more in line with our superpower.

CHAPTER 38

IKIGAI

Since my discussion with Tucker, I have found the theory of self-fulfillment articulated beautifully in the Japanese concept of *ikigai*, which means "reason for being." *Ikigai* is the intersection of what you love with what the world needs, what you can be paid for, and what you're good at.

I am constantly looking for ways that my mission, passion, profession, and vocation can intersect. Many people will recommend that you do what you have to do until you can do what you want to do. I understand that. Many of us have responsibilities and can't simply walk away from jobs that don't fulfill our passion. However, simply being aware of where you are in your life compared to where you ultimately want to go is the first step to arriving at your intended destination.

生き甲斐

Ikigai | a Japanese concept meaning "a reason for being"

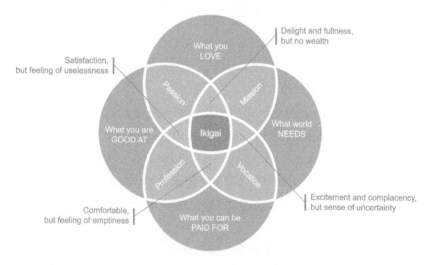

Olga Tagaeva/Shutterstock.com

CHAPTER 39

HOW TO GET HIRED

After my termination post hit Twitter, it was Froggy from *The Elvis Duran Show* who reached out and helped book me on the show. Afterward, he asked if I could meet with his wife, Lisa, to help get her résumé in order and get her motivated to find a job. I jumped at the chance!

Like so many people, Lisa had been out of work for a while and felt overwhelmed by the idea of having to start the job search all over again. We started by finding answers to the simplest questions: What do you enjoy doing? What are you good at? What kind of businesses get you excited when you speak about them? Which businesses bore you? Understanding this basic information is helpful in narrowing down potential industries to target during your job search. Think *ikigai*.

Once we narrowed things down based on her interest

level and own unique talents, we turned our attention to her résumé. The first thing we did was pull up other résumés in that industry to see what a strong résumé looked like. Highlighting your achievements and using action words when describing those accomplishments helps you create a strong résumé. Don't overthink it. You want to be thorough and create a quality document, but mulling things over too long and letting time pass you by while striving for perfection is a waste. Getting something done and out there is what will allow you to move forward. I know the process is overwhelming, so I break it down into productive steps.

1. GET REAL

Be honest with yourself. If you have been unemployed for a while, take a close look at why that is. Is it a lack of self-confidence? Are you sabotaging your own success because you don't believe you deserve it? So many people hold themselves back without even realizing it. The process is stressful and difficult enough. Don't make it harder on yourself by creating unnecessary obstacles. Identify your cop-out so you can overcome it.

2. ELIMINATE ALL DISTRACTIONS

We face countless distractions every single day that stand between us and our goals. Many of those distractions are other people. If you have people in your life who are negative or holding you back, don't be afraid to fire those people. You need people who support and understand you in your corner so you can be productive and get your work done. Life is short, so don't waste your time. Once you get rid of all the outside distractions, you can narrow your focus and take your game up a notch when going after the job you want. Be relentless and go after every available opportunity.

3. CREATE A DAILY TO-DO LIST

Not only write a to-do list every day, but also cater it specifically to your goals. Try to make progress every single day. You'd want to do the same thing if you had a job and your goal was getting promoted or doubling your income. Breaking down that bigger overall goal into smaller mini-goals and steps that you can chip away at a little each day will add up over time. Keep yourself accountable and follow through. Leave yourself reminders if you need to. I put reminders on my desk and in my phone. The more you are reminded of your end goal, the more it will become natural for you to push yourself in order to achieve that goal. Remember that those who deal in specifics seldom fail and those who deal in generalities seldom succeed. Polish your résumé and get it out there. If you've done your homework and you're religious about putting in the effort, you will get opportunities to interview. Don't let up. You're only halfway there. Keep your foot on the gas.

4. APPEARANCE MATTERS

I'm not saying every woman needs to starve herself or spend a ton of money on a Versace suit. I mean that nobody wants to hire a sloppy, disheveled person, nor does anyone want to hire a woman who comes into a professional environment looking like she is going to a nightclub. Even if a girl looks great in that outfit, it can be distracting from the real reason she is there while overshadowing her mind and abilities. Do your research and learn what company culture is all about. Some of the new tech start-ups definitely favor a more relaxed and creative vibe. If you're chasing down a specific company, try to find pictures of their offices and see how the employees dress. Speak to some of them if possible to get more information about the culture and suitable attire. Taking care of yourself mentally and physically is also a necessity. Again, this doesn't mean you need to be a certain size. It means that you need to have self-respect and take care of yourself. I always default to a pencil skirt suit or a dark pantsuit. You want to be yourself at all times, and if that means you spice up your business attire with a colorful pair of earrings, so be it. Look polished, professional, and pulled together. You don't want to walk into an interview and find that you're underdressed compared to the person interviewing you. Remember to dress the way you want to be addressed.

5. BE A SOCIAL MEDIA STALKER

You don't want to literally stalk someone because that would just be weird. What I'm suggesting is that you spend an inordinate amount of time finding out all you can about your target company. Learn about the employees and, most importantly, the hiring manager. Thankfully, Google has made this exponentially easier to do. It can be a game changer, but very few people take the time to complete this step. Learn all you can about pending projects, company awards, and the founder of the company. I like to review key managers' profiles on LinkedIn to see what we might have in common. Did they go to a Big Ten school like you? Do they have kids the same age? Did they grow up in the Northeast or major in business like you? Find common ground and bring it up in the interview. This makes the process more about the interviewer and shows that you have an interest in them. This goes far in getting potential employers to like you and helps separate you from the other candidates. There is always something there. You just need to take the time to find it.

6. CONNECT

What if you're still having trouble landing an interview?

Don't ever send in a résumé to a hiring manager and just expect to hear a response. Managers receive hundreds, possibly thousands, of résumé every day. It's a daunting and tedious task to review the dredge of standard résumés that are overflowing from any manager's inbox. The candidates who stand out when submitting to me are the ones who did their homework and contacted someone in my inner circle. I have *never* had someone ask me to do them a favor by interviewing a specific candidate and not done it. It's good business to do favors for people, and the hiring managers you're sending your résumé to will think the same way. You'll be able to see on LinkedIn or Facebook contacts you have in common. Pursue those people and see if they can get you a meeting. This works like a charm.

7. PLAN B

Everyone needs a plan B in life, and if you aren't able to find any contacts in common with the hiring manager or the person you're interviewing with (which I find hard to believe and suggest you revisit steps 5 and 6), you need to switch gears. Dive back into your research. Find out who this person is you're meeting with, and prepare what you're going to send them directly. Yes, you're going to send them something. Once, I was unable to get a meeting with a very important man in government whom I needed to see in order to pitch an idea. After a week of not getting a response to any of my emails or calls, I decided to send him something. He had a very strong Irish name. I spent time researching his family name and found his Irish family crest, so I sent him an email with the subject line, "Our crests are so similar!" In the email, I talked about how unique his family crest was and how I wished I had one like his. I received a response from him an hour later, and this led to a face-to-face meeting the following week. You are going to send the hiring manager something. It might be a video message from you. It might be a calming essence with a note saying, "I'm sorry we haven't met yet, but I want to alleviate you of the responsibility of going through countless average résumé, so I sent you this calming essence to help you get through your difficult day. Whenever you have time to see me, I will be there. I am the candidate you are looking for." Plan B is about separating yourself from the sea of mediocrity out there.

8. PRACTICE

It always shocks me when a potential candidate goes into an interview without numerous copies of a résumé available for any of the other managers who might join that meeting. It's equally shocking when candidates don't bring examples of their work or references to share. That is not how you sell yourself. An interview is about selling yourself, so you need to be prepared. The responsibility is on you as the candidate to be able to answer basic interview questions. Write them down on a piece of paper and memorize them. That may be painful, but it will increase your ability to retain the information tenfold. Use stories from your career or school to illustrate a point. The more time and thought you put into preparing for potential interview questions, the more likely that you can blow the manager away.

9. UNIQUE VALUE PROPOSITION

In order to differentiate yourself from the other candidates that made it to the face-to-face interview, you need to articulate what specifically it is that makes you unique. Why are you the obvious hire for this position? If you don't yet know what this quality is, map out your strengths and assets and compare them to what the company is looking for. It is imperative that you find a way to align your talents with their needs in order to illustrate why you're the right fit. If you're still struggling to find what makes you unique, reach out to other women you work with. Find a cross-section of people in your life and ask them to give you two specific things they think make you unique. Many women don't realize how unique they are until someone else points it out. This can be a positive and eye-opening exercise that allows you to see how special you are.

10. BE ALL ABOUT THE COMPANY

No one wants a potential candidate to come in and talk

only about themselves. Every employer looks for candidates who work well with others and can work well as a team. They want people who are collaborative and good listeners. This is how women can excel because as women we are typically interested in learning about others. Remember the connection points that you found earlier? Use those to better align yourself with the hiring manager. People like to talk about themselves, so give them this opportunity.

11. ASK THE RIGHT QUESTIONS

Be direct. You won't get the information you need to close this deal if you don't ask direct questions. I've seen many women get nervous during this phase, even when they're qualified for the job. If you're one of those women, refer back to that list of accomplishments from your journal and read about the times you exceeded expectations. Sometimes it's as simple as remembering that I completed a workout at a speed on the treadmill I once thought impossible. Once you're ready, some good direct questions to ask are, "How do I compare to your other candidates?"; "What's the skill set of the ideal candidate?"; "What happened to the person who previously had this job?"; "What would I be able to expect from you as a boss?" The more information you have, the better equipped you will be for the next step.

12. GO FOR THE CLOSE

No one will get a job if they don't go for the close. This means don't leave the office of the hiring manager without coming right out and saying, "What else do you need to know about me in order to offer me this job?" You can frame this up many different ways, but the bottom line is this: you need to ask for the offer. Do not leave that office without asking. Even if you aren't hired on the spot, this lets the manager know your level of interest.

13. FOLLOW UP

Following up is critical but can be intimidating. Women wonder if they will be perceived as a pest if they follow up too strongly. I don't agree with that. Think if the roles were reversed. Someone who is not aggressive when following up with me probably won't be aggressive when it comes to getting their work done. It's important to let the interviewer know that you appreciated his or her time. Remind that person how qualified you are for the position. Use the manager's own words in the follow-up email if possible, and ask when you can expect to hear back from them. For all they know, you have two other job offers pending, so let them know that timing is important to you.

CHAPTER 40

COUNTDOWN TO BLASTOFF

When my son recently told me that he won the student council election, it reminded me how important it was to not hesitate and just go after what we want.

I helped him with his speech. It wasn't perfect, and with Hurricane Irma fast approaching, the school moved up the date of the election, so we weren't able to get his posters done in time. However, he walked home from school that day and told me that he had won. He was a confident guy, so I wasn't surprised, but I had to ask him how he got the votes. "Was it a popularity contest? Was your speech the funniest?" No. He admitted that he wasn't the most popular kid and that another boy had the best speech. "What, then?" It turned out that he went to each one of his friends individually and had them ask others to vote for him. He also promised kids different things in exchange for votes, and they gladly obliged. In other words, he campaigned for himself, and he won. He didn't hesitate. He just asked for what he needed.

How often do you campaign for yourself? If you went out and asked individual people for help with just one thing, you would get closer to your overall goal. Why don't we do this? What do we have to lose? So many people hesitate and don't take action when deep down inside they really want to. Before they know it, the moment has passed them by and the opportunity is gone.

This phenomenon has been written about in *The 5 Second Rule* by Mel Robbins. Her book is about taking action when your inner voice speaks. The way to do that is to count backward from five. When you reach one, you take action. Robbins explains how she once struggled to get out of bed in the morning and make lunch for her kids to take to school. One night on television, she saw a shuttle getting ready for takeoff. They counted down from five before blasting off. That simple strategy was what blasted her out of bed and catapulted her into becoming an expert in taking action.

For me, taking action is not my personal challenge. The opposite is true, and oftentimes I'm told that I move too fast. "Measure twice and cut once" is a saying I heard a lot, but looking back I realize that I've been applying my own version of Robbins's strategy. Ha! Can you imagine that? One of the things that has made me confident and successful is that I've taken action when others told me not to. Listening to ourselves before we take the advice of those around us will always yield the right answer.

I've found myself using Robbins's strategy when I'm trying to get my son to go to bed. I also noticed that in spin class, when the instructor tells us to add more torque to the bike, they count us down to take action. There are countless examples when I've taken action, but I'm always prouder to share the times I've seen my son do it.

One story that stands out was when we traveled to Los Angeles recently. I had to attend work meetings, so I asked my friend Nikki to stay with us at the hotel so she could watch Dylan while I was working. When I returned to the hotel at night, I saw hundreds of young kids swarming the valet area. It turned out Justin Bieber was inside. Now, my son was obsessed with Justin Bieber, so it was no surprise that by the time I reached Dylan and Nikki, they had already combed the Montage Hotel looking for him. That went on for another two hours before Nikki and I had to convince Dylan to give up so we could go to dinner. There was no chance Bieber was going to surface with so many fans swarming outside.

We had missed our reservation at DelFrisco's because we were stalking the Biebs, and I knew they would be fully booked, so it was time to show off my skills. I walked up to the maître d' and apologized profusely for being late and let him know that my ten-year-old son had been holding us hostage at the Montage while he searched for JB. I gushed over the DelFrisco's I visited in New York City and promised that we'd be quick if he could help get us a table. He laughed. Not only did he have a table, but he had one right next to Justin Bieber, who happened to be dining in the restaurant at that exact time. We just had to promise not to bother him.

My son could barely eat. He tried to play it cool and not look, but he radiated with pure excitement. When the waiter brought JB his check, my son stood up and walked out of the restaurant. I knew what he was doing. He didn't want to bother JB while he ate like he promised but did want to grab a selfie with him outside of the restaurant. Dylan returned a few minutes later and told us that he spoke to Justin, and even though he couldn't take any pictures because the paparazzi was everywhere, he was happy to give him a hug.

Taking action without overthinking or strategizing was the only reason Dylan was able to catch Justin in that small window between finishing dinner and disappearing again for the night. Sometimes in life we have only a small window to act, so count yourself down and make your move before you miss it. The only real failure is doing nothing at all.

PART 7

. . . .

ASKING
FOR HELP

CHAPTER 41

NOBODY DOES IT ALONE

I don't have many memories of being a young girl. Those memories I do have aren't very pleasant, so I learned to block some of them out when I was younger. Repressing memories is a way we protect ourselves from what we don't want to see. This was one of the ways I coped with my difficult childhood until I was strong enough to handle it head-on.

One memory that I have is of being in fourth grade and walking home from school while a boy in my class heckled me in front of all the other kids who lived on my street. That had been happening for weeks and I was sick of it, so I decided to stand up to him. When I did, he hit me in the face. Literally, he punched me right in the face. I just remember my face feeling hot. Then I started to cry. Nobody did anything. In that moment, I felt scared and completely alone. I ran all the way home and didn't tell a soul what had happened. I didn't want to deal with the problem anymore. I just wanted it to go away.

That was a pivotal moment for me because that day I made the decision that I would no longer stand up for myself because I didn't want something like that to happen again. I never asked for help. I kept my problems to myself. The more I isolated myself, the more I thought I was doing the right thing. What I didn't know at the time was that the situation with the boy in my class was an isolated incident. I took the wrong lesson from it because standing up for myself as I did was actually the right thing to do. Unfortunately, that negative way of thinking stuck with me until my twenties. I suffered in silence. That left me feeling abandoned and alone. I didn't trust other people.

Years later, when I was driving in Michigan for my new job, I looked at myself in the rearview mirror and said, "You can count on you and that's it." While I genuinely thought I was reassuring myself, I was also closing that door to the idea of accepting help from others. If you've ever been hurt by someone, you can probably relate, but I took that feeling to another level.

When I found myself on my own in Michigan, I dived into work. I wouldn't take vacations because I didn't trust anyone to get anything done in my absence. I was also secretly scared that someone would have the chance to outperform me. That was my insecurity holding me back. The idea of being vulnerable and letting others know I needed their help with something I couldn't do on my own scared me to death. And when I acted as though I didn't need anyone's help, people stopped asking. Everyone assumed that I was tough and could get through anything. I used to think of that as a sign of strength, but today I see it as being very weak. I was setting myself up for failure.

It was around Christmas that I made the decision to fire our business manager because she was inept and needed to go. Instead of conducting a thorough search to find a quality replacement, I terminated the woman knowing that I would pick up the slack and do both her job and mine until I found someone better. Not a good decision. That Christmas, I lived at the office and was beginning to learn a very tough lesson, but it would be years before I truly felt comfortable relying on others.

Today, I know that strong people are the ones who ask for help. As with anything, how you do it is equally important. At the office, I put the project or the objective first. It does me no good to struggle alone and miss a deadline because the company suffers. If I see a problem ahead of time, I address it with my supervisor to ensure things run smoothly. One tip when asking for help at work is to offer solutions and suggestions. I not only approach my boss with the problem, but I provide a few different solutions as well. That shows I've thought things through and am challenging myself to find the answer on my own. It also allows my boss to steer me in the right direction. If you approach your boss the right way, it will be a positive that shows how you are a responsible employee who cares about getting things done right.

CHAPTER 42

BEING ASSERTIVE CAN BE BEAUTIFUL

Asking for something isn't always easy, so you want to be prepared. Once again, how you ask is just as important as what you ask, and you want to be assertive when asking for something. What does being assertive mean? Assertiveness is about being confident and demonstrating a forceful personality. That doesn't sound bad, does it? It certainly doesn't sound like something we need to apologize for or steer clear of. Instead, it sounds like something that can help us own our superpowers and move ahead. Whenever asking for something, you want to make sure that you're assertive. Here's what I do.

1. KNOW YOUR AUDIENCE

As with anything, it's critical to be familiar with your

audience before you ask for something. While I am very assertive at work, I always consider whom I'm meeting with and what's important to them before I approach. By being mindful of the unique interests of the person I'm dealing with, I can tailor my approach to fit that person's needs. This allows me to make my needs relevant to others.

2. KNOW YOUR MATERIAL

The better prepared you are, the more difficult it will be to challenge you. Often, women who are perceived as difficult at work are viewed that way because they argue from an emotional place instead of having an informed point of view on the subject matter. I do my best to be overly prepared so I can rely on facts if a conversation takes an intense turn. By remaining confident in my knowledge of the material, I am able to maintain my assertiveness when things become difficult.

3. USE YOUR STRENGTHS TO YOUR ADVANTAGE

I have the ability to connect with others, and I use that ability to my advantage. I am mindful of things such as smiling, shaking hands, and asking about someone's family when I meet with them. That's my particular power, and by standing in that power, I'm using my own attributes to my advantage. This builds confidence. What are your strengths, and how can you use them to get what you want?

4. THANK OTHERS

Be thoughtful and authentic. When you finish a meeting, it's imperative that you thank others for their time and input. It's even more important that you mean it. By being an authentic person, others will feel your warmth and transparency. That will allow them to like and trust you more. You have an advantage when others genuinely like you.

CHAPTER 43

GIVING BACK

When I received a request to do an interview with Ivanka Trump's Women Who Work website, I was very interested. The site showcased working moms and asked each of them for their tips and tricks for juggling their professional lives with parenthood. I was excited to do the interview and thought it went well, but I was very surprised to get an email from Ivanka afterward. It came from her personal email account, but it seemed as though it had been automated or cut and paste from a template that was sent to all of the women who participated in the interviews.

I found it funny, so I responded. I politely told her that I was excited to get the chance to participate but wanted her to know that the generic response didn't get customized in her email and that she might want to fix it before sending it to the next woman. Part of the reason why I responded to Ivanka and told her about the mistake was because I would want someone to do that for me. I would rather someone made me aware of a mistake so I could fix it. It might be embarrassing, but it's more embarrassing to continue making that same mistake. Ivanka was so thoughtful and kind in her response, as I believe she felt bad that I received the template response. In closing, she said if there was anything she could do to please let her know.

Years earlier, I would have let that opportunity pass me by, but now I don't hesitate to ask for help. I immediately responded and asked Ivanka if she would send out a tweet sharing my story, which is exactly what she did. When someone with 4.5 million followers tweets about you, you get some pretty interesting responses. That was an unexpected win, and it was easy. I'm sure it was something that she had no problem doing either. If the situation were reversed, I would gladly do something similar.

Asking for help is a two-way street. I'm a firm believer that you get what you give. If you're going to ask for help, you also have to be willing to help out others in return. One of the ways I like to give back is by mentoring people. Giving someone feedback and taking the time to listen to others creates such a great sense of self-worth. Paying it forward will pay off in the long run. Many of the people I've mentored over the years have gone on to succeed and then helped me in return. Some have introduced me to contacts and helped me gain access to individuals I wouldn't have been able to get through to on my own. You never know.

While doing charity work and mentoring others is an amazing way to give back, I understand that many of you don't have the time or wherewithal to do charity work. There are some very easy ways that you can help others while having the same impact. The simple act of holding the door for an elderly woman or helping a pregnant woman with her baby carriage are ways you can make a difference. There are countless times throughout the course of an average day where you will encounter someone in need of assistance. Being someone's hero can leave a lasting impact on the person you help and also yourself. That's the hidden benefit. Both parties win.

CHAPTER 44

BUILD A TEAM OF LIKE-MINDED PEOPLE

My former PR person encouraged me to write an article for a new media company called SWAAY that was launched by Iman Oubou who was Miss New York in 2015. I wrote the article, and they agreed to publish it shortly after. They were even open to reviewing and possibly publishing more articles of mine in the future.

When my relationship with that PR rep ended, I realized that my contact to SWAAY was also gone. However, I did some digging and found Iman's profile on Facebook, so I sent her a friend request. When she accepted, I sent her a DM and asked if she had time for a ten-minute call so I could ask her some questions about the TV work she had done. That was not easy for me. She was a supermodel who was twenty years younger than me. I figured she'd be wondering why I was reaching out to her.

A few days later, I actually heard back. Miss New York said she was glad to have a call with me. We talked for an hour. She was excited to hear that I was working on a concept for a show about empowering women and wanted to help any way she could. That made me feel so happy, and it shattered the idea I had in my mind of a young and gorgeous pageant winner. That one call started a friendship, and all I needed to do was reach out and ask.

Iman came at situations from a completely different perspective than I did. We each would see things the other might not notice. On my trips to New York City, we would meet for coffee or lunch to catch up. I would listen to her struggles about being an entrepreneur trying to grow her business, and she would listen to my struggles about getting fired and building my own brand from the ground up.

It was on one of those trips that she told me about a new campaign she was launching called #swaaythenarrative. The campaign was about not listening to the people who tried to put limitations on what you could achieve. I loved the idea and asked if there was any way I could be involved. I felt that I could add value to the campaign, and I wanted to get my message out there, too. Iman agreed and brought me on board. I was so excited! You can check out the interview I did for the campaign at the end of this chapter.

A few weeks later, I traveled to New York City for a group photo shoot for the campaign. I was nervous. I knew there were going to be a few models there, but I didn't realize until I got there that I would be photographed with women who were all in their twenties. I was the only one in her forties. Yikes! That was not a comfortable situation to stroll into. I let Iman know that I felt like the mother at the shoot, and she was beyond gracious. She made a point to introduce me to each woman. They were all so welcoming and encouraging. That helped me feel more confident and put me at ease. I saw the photos a few weeks later and they turned out beautiful. Letting Iman know that I needed her help opened the door for her support and assistance. That made all the difference, and I'm grateful.

I met with Iman down in Miami a few months later. We discussed her current challenges. We talked about how competitive fund-raising for a company could be and how hard it was to be taken seriously as a young woman in business. That was an issue I knew something about and could promise her that persistence and drive would pay off in the end. I realized that everyone struggles to put themselves out there when chasing their goals, regardless of what it might look like on the outside. I help her when I can, and she continues to help me. With experience,

I've learned that the people you look out for are the same people who will have your back and be honored to help you the same way. Surrounding yourself with like-minded people will keep you focused on your goals and allow you to be a part of something bigger.

* * *

HEATHER MONAHAN
43 YEARS

Currently recovering from corporate America, aka Founder of Boss in Heels

What made you choose this career path?

My entire life has led me to where I am today. Having struggled with my own insecurities early on and not having a strong female mentor led me to empower others and give them the insight I was always searching for. I feel as though this path chose me. While working in corporate America and doing what I thought I was supposed to do, I stumbled upon what I was meant to do. It didn't happen overnight. It was more of an evolution over time. As I grew more confident in myself, it became overwhelmingly clear what I needed to do. I had to be that person who I needed when I was younger. I needed to shine my light so others could see.

What has been your greatest achievement?

My greatest achievement has been becoming the person I am today for me and for my son. Always knowing that I was capable of more and not pushing myself to become better was a letdown that I didn't acknowledge until much later in life. Having a son and realizing I want him to achieve his potential helped push me to elevate myself and step into my fear in order to grow. My greatest achievement is leaving my comfort zone to achieve my potential. I try to show my son through my actions, not just my words, that everyone should chase their dreams.

Were you ever told you couldn't achieve or be something because you were too...

Absolutely. I've been told you can't go for a job that doesn't exist. You can't be a strong female without being a bitch. You can't be a mom and break the glass ceiling. You can't dress feminine and be taken seriously. I spent years being told that I should be more conservative. The ironic thing is that in the past year, as I have launched my personal brand to empower others, I have heard so much positive feedback about how others can relate to me and appreciate that I have my own sense of style and am not a canned image that would typically be seen in the board room. Believing in yourself and being yourself will always pay dividends in the end but isn't always easy along the way. Be true to you.

What is the biggest stereotype/limitation you have constantly faced when pursuing your career dreams?

My own self-doubt. If you don't have self-doubt, then it really doesn't matter what other people think or say to try to limit you.

Do you have an anecdote you can share?

Take action and develop your confidence muscle. Take action and move through fear. Who you surround yourself with is everything—fire negative people in your life and watch yourself take off. How you see yourself is how others will see you, so speak kindly to yourself, make yourself a priority, and love yourself the same way you would a baby. This takes practice, but it can become a habit. Journal to see how far you have come, and keep track of all of your small wins. Turn scarcity into abundance by writing down three things a day that you are grateful for. Moving into your fear and realizing that you are OK will give you strength for your next challenge. Backing down does the opposite. Remove the mask and become your true self. The more you can speak your real thoughts and be authentic, the stronger you will become. Speak up in meetings. Speak up for yourself, and speak your truth. Doing what you love and spending time working on your superpowers will help you feel your best every day. Becoming your number one cheerleader instead of your biggest saboteur will change your life. The moment you accept that this life is what you have created, and not what you have been given, you can take ownership and empower yourself to create change. Go for it!

How did you #swaaythenarrative?

Early on in my career, I would see an opportunity for a position that didn't exist, and while others would tell me that it was stupid, I would still pitch my idea to create a job that I felt I could fill. I did it in my first job out of college when I worked in the wine business as a sales rep. I pitched myself to be the brand manager for the state and was awarded the job. When I went to a publicly traded media company, I pitched myself for a job I thought the company needed—VP of sales. I ultimately got that job and then pitched myself for EVP of sales a few years later. After being awarded that position, I pitched myself for CRO, which I eventually got. Through all of that, I realized I had a passion for empowering others, and I created my newest role as the founder of #bossinheels. Staying focused on what I wanted, regardless of what others would say, kept me vigilant in positioning and pitching myself for opportunities that I could create.

What's your number one piece of advice for women discouraged by preconceived notions and society's limitations?

The only limitations that can be put on you are the ones that you put on yourself. Make a conscious choice to NOT put limitations on yourself and instead challenge the status quo. I love the story that Oprah was fired from TV only to rise up and become the media maven that she is today. Everyone will be told no and be told why something won't work. We're all told why we're wrong or not good enough, but those are the moments we have to pivot and find a way to make it work in spite of the negativity. If success was easy, everyone would have it. Let nothing stop you from chasing your dreams, and nothing will.

CHAPTER 45

HOW TO NETWORK LIKE AN ALL-STAR

Had I not fine-tuned my networking skills, I would have never met with Iman. So often in business and in life, we have to find our own way and create our own opportunities. You don't want to rely on luck. You want to put yourself in the best possible position to succeed, and one way to do that is through your contacts and who you know.

The secret to being a good networker at events and in a social setting is to smile and walk up to people with an extended hand. It truly is that simple. The reality is that everyone is just as uncomfortable as you are, so breaking through that initial awkwardness will always be received warmly. What's the worst that can happen? No one is going to throw a drink at you for introducing yourself or making small talk. On the upside, you might meet a great new contact. Here are several basic rules to get you started.

1. OPEN WITH A COMPLIMENT

I like to think of one way that I can compliment someone when I approach. People love to talk about themselves and they love authentic compliments. If I can't think of anything, I'll poke fun at the venue or joke about some innocent topic we both relate to. One of my favorite lines is, "Gotta love another 6:00 p.m. cocktail party for charity." I'll ask if they have kids, or how they juggle everything. By being conversational and interested in the other person, you make connections much easier.

2. DON'T MAKE IT UNCOMFORTABLE

This seems like a no-brainer, but it's easy to fall into this trap if you aren't careful. If you're approaching a powerful person, be aware that you aren't the only one doing so. The trick is to approach that person in a thoughtful way that shows your value. Do your homework on your target if possible. Read their blog, familiarize yourself with their work, and learn what they are most proud of. There are very few people in this world who are put off by someone who approaches with positive feedback on their work. Once again, don't make the conversation about you, and you will make a good first impression.

3. BE AWARE OF BODY LANGUAGE

You have to look the part. Always dress for the job, and be sure to put your best foot forward. When I know that I'm going to an event or will have the opportunity to meet other people, I take extra time to get myself ready. Pick out your best outfit. Find your strongest color and the shoes that make you feel on-point. This will allow you to bring your most confident self to the exchange. Be sure to keep your head held high. Make eye contact and smile. It all comes down to nailing those first ten seconds because that is all the time it takes for the other person to decide if they will engage with you or not.

4. STAY OPTIMISTIC

Make sure you keep a positive attitude. Convince yourself that your meeting with a powerful person will turn out fantastic. My favorite tactic is to remind myself of a time when I surprised myself. I refer to my journal once again and go back to that list to see when I was able to pull something off that I didn't think I could. You'll be reminded that good can come out of any situation if you go in with a positive attitude. The worst that can happen is that you won't be able to engage in a conversation. So what? That means you have more time to meet someone who is interested.

5. YOU CAN'T SUCCEED EVERY TIME

Don't get down if one person doesn't want to speak with you. It's so easy to lose your positive attitude or to give up. Instead, I like to give myself a goal of introducing myself to a minimum of five people in any given situation. That way, I can't walk out early or feel defeated if something doesn't go my way right out of the gate. If you follow through and make five introductions, I promise you that one of them will pan out. It's a numbers game.

6. DON'T LINGER WITH ONE CONTACT

One of the biggest traps people fall into is attending an event and having a great conversation with someone you don't want to stop talking to. Be sure to always leave people wanting more from you, rather than wanting to leave you because you talked their ear off. I give myself a finite period to talk with someone before I excuse myself. I like to have reasons ready to excuse myself from conversations so I can move on to my next target. It's simple. Say you have to use the ladies' room or grab a drink.

7. REMEMBER NAMES

One of the ways I remember people's names when going into an event is I use word association. If I meet a woman named Alicia, I find ways to associate her with Alicia Keys so that her name will instantly pop into my mind when

I run into her again. People love it when you remember their name, so make it a game and associate everyone you meet with someone you will remember.

8. FOLLOW UP

Later that night or the following day, it's important to email or reach out to your contacts through LinkedIn. Thank them for their time, and try to set up a follow-up meeting. Once you have that initial meeting under your belt, the follow-up is always much easier.

Practice makes perfect. The more you practice your networking skills, the better you will become and the faster your network will grow.

AFTERWORD

My good friend Rafe has been asking me to write a book for years. He saw the way that I was able to succeed at work while going through a divorce and raising a wonderful boy and felt that my story would inspire other women to realize their potential if they just went after it.

Rafe wasn't the only one telling me this. I've traveled extensively over the past decade, so I've gotten to know just about everyone who works at the Miami airport. There was one man who I always saw every time I was there. We'd exchange pleasantries and small talk, but one day he caught me off guard when telling me that I was different from the other women he crossed paths with at the airport. He liked how I was always trying. What he meant was that I wouldn't come to the airport in sweatpants. I always did my hair and had a nice outfit on. He told me that when I arrived at the airport, it looked like I was getting ready for the runway, and he loved that about me. He said that I should write a book about how to become your best self.

When you notice multiple friends and family members telling you the same thing over and over again, listen to them. I used to laugh when people would talk to me about writing a book, but the more I thought about it, the more I liked the idea. However, it's one thing to want to write a book and another thing to actually do it. I constantly told myself that I didn't have enough time. That was my cop-out. But why didn't I have the time? The problem was that so much of my time was spent making everyone else's priorities my top priority. Why not put myself first? Once I decided to make the book my priority, all of those excuses disappeared.

When it came time to execute, I faced a different set of challenges. I was completely overwhelmed because the task felt massive. The first thing I did was watch an online tutorial on how to write a book. That sounds crazy, but there is so much to learn when tapping into the experience of others who have been there before. What I learned from watching that tutorial was that the most important thing to do was to sit down and start writing. Taking action was the key, so that's what I did. I started with small steps. I broke down what felt like a huge endeavor into more manageable goals that I could accomplish easily. That allowed me to feel good about myself in the process.

I knew that I couldn't do it alone. It was important to let those closest to me know what I was doing and ask for their help. My friends and family proved invaluable when reminding me of stories that I had forgotten and helping me find an editor. Leaning on the good people in my life and asking for their help paid off. It also held me accountable to myself and others once I shared my commitment with the people I trusted. That forced me to keep going and not turn back.

Opening up was difficult. Many times since I've started writing, I've thought about what the haters were going to say. As with so many things in life, facing fear is the real challenge. The fear of what others will think or say. The fear of hurting those close to me. The fear of failure. All of those fears were staring me in the face every single day I worked on this project, but I knew that everything I wanted was on the other side of that fear. That was what propelled me to charge forward and finish this book.

I hope that you find something in this book that can help you as much as the experience helped me. If I can teach just one person how to build their confidence and realize they are not alone when struggling through life, then this was all worth it. I wish you all the best of luck. We are all in this together, so please keep me updated on your success!

Check out my social media feeds for daily inspo @heathermonahan, and sign up for my newsletter on my website www.heathermonahan.com.

ACKNOWLEDGMENTS

I'd like to thank following people that contributed to the book including my editor Ryan Dempsey, my photographer Jessielyn Palumbo and my fiancé for making this happen.

ABOUT THE AUTHOR

Growing up in a trailer with her mother and three siblings, **HEATHER MONAHAN** lacked self-confidence. She had no self-esteem and was not the person she aspired to be. Over time, that changed, and she is living proof that confidence is not born, but learned. Heather has since dedicated her life to empowering others by pulling back the curtain to reveal what it takes to get ahead at work and in life. Heather launched Boss In Heels, a global community and a lifestyle brand dedicated to helping others gain confidence and live the life they want to live.

CPSIA information can be obtained
at www.ICGtesting.com
Printed in the USA
BVHW030123271018
531315BV00001B/1/P